Fictional Truth

PARALLAX RE-VISIONS OF CULTURE AND SOCIETY
Stephen G. Nichols, Gerald Prince, and Wendy Steiner,
series editors

FICTIONAL TRUTH

MICHAEL RIFFATERRE

The Johns Hopkins University Press
Baltimore and London

For Hermine

© 1990 The Johns Hopkins University Press
All rights reserved
Printed in the United States of America

The Johns Hopkins University Press
701 West 40th Street
Baltimore, Maryland 21211
The Johns Hopkins Press Ltd., London

The paper used in this publication meets the minimum require-
ments of American National Standard for Information Sciences—
Permanence of Paper for Printed Library Materials,
ANSI Z39.48-1984

Library of Congress Cataloging-in-Publication Data
will be found on the last printed page of this book.

Contents

Foreword

In *Fictional Truth* Michael Riffaterre has written a model of the speculative essay which it is one of the goals of this series to make available. At the same time, the book embodies the dual perspective on a problem of cultural study represented by the series title.

Riffaterre defines realism, the master mode of nineteenth- and early twentieth-century fiction, in terms of its basic paradox: it is true because fictional, realistic because removed from life. Arguing that truth is primarily a matter of linguistic perception, a triumph of semiosis over mimesis, that the truth of fiction lies in its rhetorical power, not in its likeness to reality, Riffaterre challenges a premise of current critical orthodoxy: formalism has little or nothing to teach us about literature's access to historical context.

In so doing he vigorously espouses a fundamental philosophical proposition regarding the way in which language represents truth by substituting an idea of truth for an experience of actuality. For Riffaterre, the lesson, and the paradox, of nineteenth-century realism lies in its rejection of simple referentiality. He offers an historical corrective to the reigning critical orthodoxy that accepts referentiality as the principal—in some critics the only—legitimate form of art's interaction with the social formation that produced it. In speaking of the "shackles of referentiality," he reminds us that high realism did not simply seek to chronicle its historical moment, but sought to develop a more scientific means for representing truths freed from the distortions of punctual relativism.

In studying the mechanisms of that search for a more accurate process of representing, Riffaterre carefully situates his project in an historical continuum. The painter Delacroix, for example, rejected Balzac's obsession for realistic details in his writing as an immersion in minutia passing for mimetic truth: "What is the use of giving full-length portraits of so many secondary characters that all interest of the book disappears?" Delacroix recognizes that attempts to present truth as mimesis can lead to a narrative abyss. Or, as Nelson Goodman remarks, "The whole truth would be too much; it is too vast, variable, and clogged with trivia." It is also relativistic.

Explicitly rejecting the traditional link between realism and minute observation of the world, the somewhat literal concept of mimetic truth, Riffaterre shows how the rhetorical forces at work in realistic narrative play off the reader's knowledge of historical context through linguistic patterns of verisimilitude. Fiction establishes its *truth* status by the way language turns back upon itself, tautologically, to accomplish the expectations it sets up. The narrative need not be judged true because it corresponds to an external image of the world, but because it is consistent with the linguistic usages current in a given social context, at a given moment in time.

Riffaterre seeks to show how fiction in the modern era organized the master tropes through which it represented its own social and political fabric as narrative object. He shows us the rhetorical givens and the philosophical presuppositions, as well as the preoccupation with socially differentiated linguistic registers underlying high-cultural fiction. We are taken behind the scenes of artistic production and the workings of social vision—"worldmaking" as Nelson Goodman puts it—are revealed to us in ways that may finally be more revealing than some kinds of politically oriented literary criticism.

If the oxymoron of the title underscores the paradoxical relationship of modernist fiction to its context, it also marks a continuity with a millennial tradition of storytelling that modernism's emphasis on realism as a mode often obscures. With the oxymoron, *fictional truth*, Riffaterre restates in modern terms a universal verbal representation, articulated even by philosophers of the Middle Ages, as a means of joining history, theory, and language to describe the principle of abstract conjecturality as a ground for representing the world.

When Johns Scottus Eriugena reflected on language in the ninth century, he recognized that the hidden nature of the sign, its abstract conjecturality (what Borges or Umberto Eco call its labyrinthine quality) made it a semiotic rather than simply a mimetic phenomenon. In a metaphor that brilliantly conveys the distance between sign and referent, he identified the gap that determines the conjectural nature of language. Citing the example of a fountain, he reasoned that it is not at the outlet that the water comes into being; it originates elsewhere, out of sight, and much further away in hidden springs. The metaphor of the fountain served Eriugena not as the symbol of origin, but rather as proof of the differentiating flux of representation.

Like Riffaterre, Eriugena made the human mind the locus for perceiving and representing the world. Since all forms of expression will be mediated through the mind, there can be no question of naïve mimetic realism. The metaphor of the fountain incorporates an awareness of the parallax factor that teaches the distortions inherent in perception. The image of the real and apparent sources of the water flowing from the fountain conveys the principle of differentiation by which things in the world divide, diversify, and become opaque.

Eriugena identified two kinds of master narratives, the one historical and the other symbolic. Both argue the mediated nature of language that makes narrative a record of the mind's perception of the world rather than a direct representation of external reality. We can already see in Eriugena the paradox of reality represented in fictional narrative: diegesis serving as truth. The two master tropes are "mystery," Eriugena's term for historical narrative, and "symbol," or didactic genres. Recollected events in the world, history, are mysteries because they are ultimately unknowable in any complete sense. They may only be partially recovered and then only in narratives that become conflated with the event itself. All historical narrative is thus allegory, an allegory grounded in event but recounted in words. He uses the term mystery to encompass the allegory of word and event to remind us of the element of absence, of incompletion in any historical account; and allegory, of the same reason Riffaterre speaks of "fictional truth." It is less the factuality of the event that matters for Eriugena than its ability to stimulate reflection *on the represented event,* the event as text. He does not downplay the element of historicity, but, as with Riffaterre, it is the diegetic process that ultimately marks both the connectedness to the world and the opacity of that link—its mystery.

Eriugena identified a second kind of allegory, an allegory of exemplarity which he identified as allegory of the word alone or symbol. Unlike mysteries, symbols are not historical events but discourses recounting things that did not happen as though they had happened for didactic purposes. In short, symbolic narrative may invent scenarios at will for the purpose of conveying truths that transcend specific situations. Eriugena, like Riffaterre, was no relativist and his narrative modes—allegory of word and deed (mystery) and allegory of word (symbol)—between them suggest that the whole purpose of writing was to translate disparate events into fictional truths.

In the medieval schema, mystery, the historical, was subordinate to symbol, reserved for transcendent truths beyond history. The service of higher truth authorized fictional scenarios since truth value lay in exemplarity, not referentiality. Indeed, the truth of the parable, Eriugena reminds us, lies precisely in its self-declaration of fictionality.

Riffaterre's *Fictional Truth* has impressive cultural roots. These roots corroborate his insights in attributing the social imaging for which realism is justly renowned not to the more perfect mirroring of external reality, but to the superior rhetorical and intertextual manipulation of *le mot juste*.

STEPHEN G. NICHOLS
University of Pennsylvania

Acknowledgments

The analytical approach to the fictionality of fiction that I propose in these pages was first sketched in my 1987 seminar on narrative diegesis at the School of Criticism and Theory at Dartmouth. It further developed in my course on literary theory at Columbia, and was later formalized in lectures that I gave last year as a Fellow of the Center for Cultural Studies of the University of Pennsylvania. I am especially indebted to Professor Stephen G. Nichols for his encouragement and friendly comments. I owe much to the attention to detail and critical acumen of my assistants, Isabelle Chagnon, Carol Howard, and Elisabeth Ladenson.

Introduction

All literary genres are artifacts, but none more blatantly so than fiction. Its very name declares its artificiality, and yet it must somehow be true to hold the interest of its readers, to tell them about experiences at once imaginary and relevant to their own lives. This paradox of truth in fiction is the problem for which I propose to seek a solution. At any rate, I propose to define those areas where an inquiry may be fruitful. There will be no attempt here at a philosophical approach, but merely a systematic scrutiny of the textual mechanisms and the verbal structures that represent or imply the truth of a fictitious tale.

It seems obvious that this scrutiny should focus on content analysis and on the forms that point to content even though they may not represent it directly. Such has not been the focus of modern narratology, which has instead emphasized narrative structures, plot typology, and the functions embodied in the personae of narrator and characters, including the impact of their viewpoints on the telling of the story rather than on the personae themselves. A taxonomy has been developed to distinguish between fictional subgenres and between fiction and other forms of literary discourse. In short, these approaches have generated abstract models and various grammars of narrative. They are less useful in explaining how the structures are actualized and how they produce concrete forms, without which there could be no reader response.

I concentrate, on the contrary, on the actualization of structures, the ways in which models are fleshed out with the description of characters and settings, and the representations of the thoughts and speech of these characters. In short, I am concerned here with the *diegetic* implementation of narrative models, which is achieved through the complementarity of the narrative and of the descriptive, a mutual dependency that can roughly be expressed by saying that the syntax is narrative and its lexicon, descriptive. The solution of the truth-in-fiction paradox evidently lies in redefining referentiality. Whereas referentiality assumes an actual or potential relationship between language and reality, we have to hypothesize that this assumption suffices only so long as it respects the rules of representation that exist in any language and with which all speakers of that language are familiar. Words may lie yet still tell a truth if the rules are followed.

My first chapter makes the case that truth in fiction is not based on an actual experience of factuality, nor does the interpretation or esthetic evaluation of fictional narrative require that it be verified against reality. Rather, truth in fiction rests on verisimilitude, a system of representations that seems to reflect a reality external to the text, but only because it conforms to a grammar. Narrative truth is an idea of truth created in accordance with the rules of that grammar. These rules implement a principle of substitutability: by virtue of this principle, any verbal given will seem to be true when it generates tautological derivations that repeat it in successive synonymous forms. This is because the entire narrative sequence becomes saturated with these synonyms and functions consequently like a paradigm of references to the unchanging semantic structure of the given. For each component of that structure, which is either implicit in the given or only briefly and incompletely made explicit, the derivative fictional text substitutes explicit and developed descriptions. On the one hand, in order to be grammatically correct, each of these must conform to a consensus about reality, a consensus already encoded in language. On the other hand, each of these descriptions does no more than expatiate individually on the semantic components of the same given. The combination of these multiple references to the given, of the verifiability of each against the accepted idea of reality, of the very bulk of detailed translations of each into actual descriptions, and of convergence on one initial lexical or phrasal given convey the impression of truth. Distributed on a time axis and in accordance with a logic of causality, the whole derivative text becomes equivalent to, and seems therefore the confirmation of, the initial representation. The relation between the derivation and its source is not unlike the relation between the detailed definition contained in the encyclopedic part of a dictionary entry and the word that entry is about.

Narrative truth is thus a linguistic phenomenon; since it is experienced through enactment by reading, it is a performative event in which participation on the reader's part can only serve to hammer the text's plausibility into his experience. Because of this, the verbal nature of mimesis, since the transformation of the given into synonymous representations corresponds to the conventions of a society or of a class, these also serve as guidelines for the positive or negative interpretations the reader is led to adopt. Such conventions quite visibly alter and redirect the meanings of the mimesis into ideologically motivated semiotic codes. Fiction relies on codes, that is, on arbitrary conventions that can be identified independently of the narrative, that are assignable to a viewpoint exterior to it, or that can be perceived as irrelevant to the motivation of narrative events. Because of these discrepancies, fiction emphasizes the fact of the fictionality of a story at the same time it states that the story is true. Furthermore, verisimilitude is an artifact, since it is a verbal representation of reality rather than reality itself: verisimilitude itself, therefore, entails fictionality.

Chapter 2 analyzes the mechanism of this paradoxical phenomenon. While I recognize that there are indices of fictionality that generate unusually well-structured, conspicuous narrative motivation to balance the loss of verisimilitude, more can be learned about fiction from those indices that point to narrative truth by seeming to flout it. Far from being the exception, these signs are much used, an indication of their importance. Indeed, they differentiate between literary and nonliterary narratives and may even be a locus of fiction's literariness since all of them are tropes.

These tropes generate what we feel to be a circuitous artificial version of a story that could have been told more simply. The twisted narrative cannot be understood or the point of veering away from the straight story cannot be seen without the reader's mentally rebuilding or hypothesizing a pretransformation text.

Humor is the primary trope of this kind, the most frequently employed and the one whose effects may range through the whole of a novel. It clearly betrays authorial intrusion or indicates a narrator's viewpoint incompatible with verisimilitude. At the same time, the pretransformation state of the humorous narrative stands for the truth that the trope has translated into artifice. Emblematic names for characters are another case in point. The trope of which they are a variant is antonomasia. They are blatantly conventional, and yet they function as givens, of the kind I discuss in the previous chapter, from which a tautological derivation issues that verifies repeatedly an initial representation. The only difference is that the derivation here amplifies on a name that constitutes a program for its bearer's life, or that limits that life to one revealing behavior, or that spells out the implications of the psychological or social type the emblem stands for.

With Chapter 3 the argument moves from truth related to verisimilitude to a qualitatively different truth related to symbolism. Language is veridictory when it parallels rather than refers to the nature of things by multiplying representations that are different yet tautological, affirming its coherence in terms of grammaticality and of consistency with the given. The truth of symbolism in fiction, by contrast, is separated from the narrative it verifies, since it is a commentary or gloss on it. This separation is none other than the divide between metalanguage and language. Difference itself is a truth-creating device, because a metalanguage functions as if it presupposed the reality of the topics it glosses, when it actually presupposes the reality of the language in which these topics are broached. Metalanguage remains the same whether it rests on an actual referentiality or is an image of referentiality. There is no formal difference between a metalinguistic reading of a text about accepted facts and that of a text whose contents are a figment of the author's imagination. Thus Rabelais's make-believe learned quotations from spurious erudite sources and Melville's mostly accurate references to cetology symbolize the truth of these authors' fictional stories equally well. Symbolic reference is convincing whether the referent is fictional or real, because the reference itself as a function (as opposed to the referent as the object of that function) is the same in both instances.

Symbolism raises the problem of the gap between the metalinguistic structure of its referentiality, the sequential telling of the story, and the hierarchy of esthetic values that make the novel into an artifact. What accounts for the bridging of the gap, it seems to me, is the presence of subtexts, texts within the text that are neither subplots nor themes but diegetic pieces whose sole function is to be vehicles of symbolism. They offer a rereading of the plot that points to its significance in a discourse closer to poetry than to narrative. The connection between the two types of discourse is established through verbal overdetermination, making up for the irrelevance of verisimilitude to metalanguage. This overdetermination consists in welding together narrative text and symbolic subtexts with two possible intermediaries: sustained metaphors, as an imagistically motivated consecution, or syllepses, as a phonetically motivated one.

The last chapter is devoted to the psychoanalytical model of truth, to the commonplace assumption that a suppressed truth must be deemed truer and that the opposition of the conscious and the unconscious parallels that between appearances and reality. *Model* is the key word here. To suppose that fictional truth could be recovered only with the help of the analyst's special expertise would be to deny literature's natural power over its readers. It seems more satisfactory to recognize that there is an unconscious of the text that works like the human unconscious. This unconscious of the text is represented by the symbolism of the subtext and by the intertext this symbolism mobilizes. Readers accede to it not by

plumbing the innermost recesses of the psyche, but by following the clues of the text itself.

There are two categories of such clues. One is the perception of constants in the narrative subtexts, the other the perception of ungrammaticalities. Constants become obvious
through a comparative reading that is dictated by the successive versions of any given subtext, and the fact that, in order
to understand each new version, readers have to rely more
and more on the previous ones. As a result, readers reach the
point at which they actually perceive structural invariants
through the layer of changing and yet synonymous representations: memory-oriented readings displace text-oriented readings, and disclose the unchanging fundamentals of significance, the points where it abuts psychic structures.

As for ungrammaticalities, they signal that the subtext's
meaning does not derive from the chain of events of the surrounding narrative, but from references to an intertext that
remains the same for each successive version of the subtext.
Recovery of the intertext demands no special expertise,
because the text itself signals its location through ungrammaticalities. These ungrammaticalities are the most effective and
conspicuous, not just because they disturb verisimilitude,
but because in a time-oriented context they focus on an
unchanging intertextuality, deriving their significance from
their reference to an intertext that has no past, no future, no
temporality, an image therefore of immovable truth – or
again, the equivalent of the locked-in unconscious that an
analyst deduces from the analysand's symptoms. Hence, a
double paradox: not only does fictional truth rest on factors
that tend to threaten verisimilitude, but it gives the narrative
the authority of the real by eliminating or suspending the
most basic feature of narrativity, its time dimension.

In studying a topic in which it is so difficult to define

basic concepts without philosophical generalizations that take us away from literary specificity, the complexity of the task is compounded by the elusiveness of the idea of truth in literary fiction, of what readers sense to be the truth of a story. I have attempted therefore to palliate these difficulties with simple models that I hope have something of the general easy applicability to the description of literature that geometry provides for the description of natural shapes. I have especially emphasized facts and concepts that are self-evident and unlikely to be blurred by the subjectivity of esthetic evaluation and hermeneutic uncertainties, the mechanics of repetition, for instance, or the imperative logic of presupposition.

I have always tried to avoid abstract theorizing but rather to test theory against close readings of fiction chosen at random from Austen to Proust, from Balzac to Henry James. A glossary of terms is meant to help students, and perhaps everybody, avoid confusion in using technical concepts that are equally relevant to literary theory and to textual analysis.

All ellipses in quotations are mine.

One

Truth in Diegesis

The only reason that the phrase "fictional truth" is not an oxymoron, as "fictitious truth" would be, is that fiction is a genre whereas lies are not. Being a genre, it rests on conventions, of which the first and perhaps only one is that fiction specifically, but not always explicitly, excludes the intention to deceive. A novel always contains signs whose function is to remind readers that the tale they are being told is imaginary.

The wonder is that fiction still manages to interest, to convince, and eventually to appear relevant to the reader's own experience, despite containing so many reminders of its artificiality. The wonder also is that it eludes the ever-present danger that the imaginary story may appear gratuitous. Furthermore, whatever symbolic truth fiction may have, that truth results from a rhetorical transformation of the narrative into figurative discourse or from situational analogies

I

between the writer's inventions and representations of recognized reality. Our task, therefore, is not just to explain interest and relevance despite fictitiousness or to show that the narrative sequence is fully motivated, and in fact overdetermined, even though it cannot be verified against real objects. We must also account for the indices that a narrative always provides to guide readers' interpretations, to prevent them from mistaking the tropological version of the diegesis for a stylistic icing on the cake. Rather, these indices point out that the story, however unreal it may be, remains relevant to readers' experience. As there are signs of fictionality, there must be signs palliating it, signs indicating a convention of truth, signs of a plausibility that makes readers react to a story as if it were true.

These signs constitute the system of verisimilitude in which students of literature traditionally see a discursive phenomenon, a special instance of mimesis. If this were the case, verisimilitude would be a modality of the diegesis, the latter being the spatial and temporal universe in which a story unfolds, the linguistic actualization of narrative structures. This view originally developed through an ethical criticism that made truth the criterion of good fiction, a truth based on a *vraisemblance* defined as a conformity with ideological models. The more recent developments of narratology take a different tack: verisimilitude is found in consecution rather than in the mimesis superimposed on it. It is therefore analyzed as a special instance of motivation, that is, as a compellingly visible coherence in the sequence of causes and effects. The two interpretations have this in common: they distinguish two signifying chains that, by developing parallel to each other, generate the narrative and descriptive sequences of a story.

I submit that the two interpretations of verisimilitude can be reconciled. They seem incompatible only because the traditional doctrine explains textual facts in terms of their relations to factors exterior to the text, whereas the newer approach sees verisimilitude in terms of relations entirely contained within the text. The former privileges the mimesis, a sign system seemingly based on the referentiality of its components, that is, on the assumption that words carry meaning by referring to things or to nonverbal entities. The latter privileges the narrative sequentiality that is entirely within the text's boundaries.

This opposition, however, is more apparent than real. In fact, exterior referentiality is but an illusion, for signs or sign systems refer to other sign systems: verbal representations in the text refer to verbal givens borrowed from the sociolect, but such verbal givens are actually present in the text, explicitly or implicitly, as presuppositions.

Thus the narrative sequence and its diegetic implementation (the mimesis) are both intratextual, since both are derivations from a given that selects simultaneously the abstract structure that serves as a model for the narrative sequence and the representation that will first actualize that structure and make it visible and readable. The reader can neither perceive nor decode the one without the other, since the narrative structural invariant must be actualized, and it is the diegetic sequence that performs this function by transforming it into concrete variants. Narrative motivation and diegetic verisimilitude must thus be seen as two facets of the same phenomenon or, better still, as complementary features of the same text. Coherent motivation is perceived as coherent for three reasons: (1) it fulfills certain expectations; (2) it follows a logic of events; and (3) at each point at which a character faces a choice in the course of actions to be undertaken, at each proairesis (Aristotle's term for such choices) motivation severely limits the number of choices. All three categories—expectations, logic, and choice-range—reflect the wisdom and experience of the readership, or rather, the prevailing ideology or ideologies that may be mobilized in assessing a situation or individual behavior. These mental frames of reference, however, are not just habits of thought; they constitute potential ministories, ready to unfold when needed and ready for reference when alluded to. The action *having a drink* or just the idea of a drink, in any narrative or indeed any conceptualization, depends on the availability of a verbal sequence: ordering and obtaining the drink (conflated into making oneself a drink, if the epic of thirst conquered is a private quest); drinking the drink with the proairesis of slow sipping, fast bottoms-up, or spilling; paying for it, and so on. Parallel to this narrative unit are valorizations with their own ready-made sequences, such as conviviality, including the option of the bartender as conscience-director, versus solitary soaking-up, etc., etc. Such sequences are essentially unchangeable orders of succession: action first, then consequences. They therefore form a syntax, a grammar of linear distribution with the *before-after* rule basic to narrative, and appropriate props like tense and conjunctions for retrograding from the end to the beginning, from the present to the past. If any lexicon comes with that syntax, it remains at the most abstract level of types or *actants* as opposed to actors.

On the other hand, lexicon is specificity itself in the diegetic sequence: there, *actants* become individualized as actors, and the syntactic ordering of the participants becomes actualized—for instance, as a place, a stage, a background—and endowed with its own representational sensory signs (picturesque, realism, and so forth). These words fill out the slots of the narrative syntax, so that we can see the two sequences narrative/syntactic and diegetic/lexical as indeed parallel, the second receiving its motivating coherence from the first.

But, as I suggested before, there is a point at which the two meet, and where the diegetic sequence partakes of the motivating function, at times coming close to taking it over. Every single word that may fill the syntactic slots contains a potential narrative and a potential diegesis, as atoms may be parts of larger universes and yet contain within themselves a similarly organized universe. Each word is a sememe, a complex system of associated semantic features or semes interrelated by their own unchanging syntax, and these semes may in turn be actualized in the shape of lexical representations, of satellite words gravitating around the term that represents the original sememe. The lexical actualizations themselves are organized by syntax, also actual, that reflects the potential one within the sememe. These actualizations form what I call a *descriptive system*. Because actualization is always possible, a sememe can be seen as an inchoate or future text, and a story as an expanded sememe in which a temporal dimension has been added to spatial syntagms. Furthermore, any element of the descriptive system has a metonymic relationship with the nuclear world. This works to the extent that, on the one hand, the nuclear word can at any time generate a story simply by transforming its implicit semes into words and letting them be organized by narrative structures, and, on the other hand, the story can be organized by the inner grammar of the sememe. In such cases, verisimilitude takes over motivation, because each word of that story will expatiate on or repeat the nuclear word that begets it, for each such word is also a metonym of that nucleus. The derivation will fulfill expectations and conform to the readership's consensus about things because it transforms into an explicit text a meaning already implicit in the generating word. Any agreement between the narrative model and the sememic model will produce a double motivation and therefore an ironclad verisimilitude.

This concept, it seems to me, explains how the same text

can be at once fictional and true, how verisimilitude can substitute an idea of truth for an actual experience of actuality, thus freeing fiction from the shackles of reference and making truth a concept that depends on grammar and is therefore impervious to change, rather than on our subjective, idiosyncratic, and changeable experience of reality.

First, let us get rid of the presumed opposition between narrative verisimilitude and narrative arbitrariness. In order to dismiss that distinction, I shall borrow the very examples with which Gérard Genette has tried to establish it.[1] Genette first distinguishes between a verisimilar narrative and an arbitrary one. Verisimilar: *The marquise* (I am preserving the French title for reasons that will become clear) *ordered her carriage and went for a drive.* Arbitrary: *The marquise ordered her carriage and went to bed.* This arbitrariness, Genette avers, is not formally, that is, syntactically, different from the verisimilar story, and they must be distinguished by virtue of a judgment that may be psychological but that is at any rate external to the text. The truly arbitrary narrative, according to Genette, will be one with explicit motivation, such as *The marquise ordered her carriage and went to bed, for she was very capricious* (or: *for she was very capricious, as all marquises are wont to be*). By contrast, her going for a drive is verisimilar, for no motivation needs to be added. In other words, Genette makes the motivation sequence start with the ordering of a carriage, not with the subject of the action. Strictly speaking, *going for a drive* is a narrative unit of the kind I exemplified with *having a drink.* But this unit is here subordinated to the descriptive system of *marquise,* and under the overriding pressure of that motivation, all three narratives are equally verisimilar, if perhaps not equally exciting.

First, *marquise* bespeaks a rank and privileges that entail the use of a carriage. Second, the sememe *marquise,* in French, emphatically comprises semes such as *caprice, spoiled*

6   FICTIONAL TRUTH

temper, and indeed *arbitrariness* to a degree unknown to other titles of nobility: *duchesse* and *comtesse* are just descriptive, *baronne* slightly parodic or nouveau riche; *marquise* still embodies the exemplary selfish and irresponsible whimsies of the Marquise de Pompadour and her decadent era. In consequence, the proairesis following *carriage availability* admits equally of two contrary options (take it or leave it), and arbitrariness is as verisimilar as conformity would be in the subjectless and therefore open narrative unit, *going for a ride.* Furthermore, explicit motivation, that is, reference to caprice, does spell out arbitrariness, but only inasmuch as that arbitrariness is a marker of truth. This is so because the text is equally motivated narratively and semiotically, as derivative syntax and as lexical derivation. In other words, verisimilitude increases (rather than decreases, as Genette would have it) as motivation goes from implicitness to explicitness and occupies more and more textual space. The improbable action is made more truly improbable as the actualized descriptive systems of *marquise* transform that noblewoman from a mere tag into a whole picture: the whole improbable act is overdetermined, since the derivation from the subject makes us expect the less expected of the two options presented by the narrative predication. Or again: verisimilitude is born of a combination of a derivation from a lexical given and a derivation from a situational given, the two deviations being one, since both transform a structure, either sememic or narrative, into the same text.

This transformation is tautological: because the story develops the given, by actualizing the given's descriptive system, the metonyms are a variation on the sememe corresponding to the given. This is my second point: narrative truth is born of tautology. As a consequence of the fact that this overdetermination is entirely contained in the text and therefore self-sufficient, and that it is an exclusively linguistic phenomenon, readers need not be familiar with the reality that the text is about in order to believe it true. The only reference against which they need to test the narrative's truth is language. All they have to verify is that the text is derived grammatically, that is to say, within the permissible equivalences between the sememe's latent text and the narrative model's possible actualizations, between a seme and the various words that may represent it, between these words and the periphrases that may be substituted for them.

These transformations, of course, are regulated by teleology. Depending as they do on the story's telos, they are meant to propound a thesis, to comply with formal esthetics selected to that end. They are therefore fictitious. Because they are overdetermined, however, they appear true, and all the truer the more textual space they occupy.

This can be tested in the most outrageously unreferential kind of veridiction: the apodeictic statements attributing a meaning or import to a narrative item, whether an event, a situation, a gesture, a facial expression, or an intonation. The assertion must be axiomatic and unverifiable. Thus, this street scene in Proust; the place is a small town, the time the late afternoon, just before vespers:

> No one yet was to be seen in front of the church except for the lady in black one sees leaving hurriedly at any given time in provincial towns.[2]

The details (the widow's weeds, the hurried steps, and the quick transition they intimate from lonely prayer to the bustle of the waiting household) individualize the character. The contrasting generality of the statement, seemingly incompatible with this particular scene, arbitrarily transforms details that should depict one person only into a pseudorule of behavior, making her a type, an actant rather than an actor. The humor of the contrast and of the arbitrary interpreta-

FICTIONAL TRUTH

tion, instead of detracting from the plausibility of the rule, challenges the reader to adopt a mood of amused rueful concession ("come to think of it, there *are* such people"). The axiomatic turn of phrase alone suffices to presuppose a truth, even though the reader's experience may not provide him with personal examples. These apodeictic statements are significantly frequent in the novels of nineteenth-century Realism. Balzac, in particular, founds the truth he claims for his fictional sociology either on descriptive details open to verification or on maxims precluding it, on the order of *One of those merciless fights as are fought in provincial life*, or *Such remarks must sound obscure to those who have not yet observed the mores peculiar to places divided into upper and lower neighborhoods* ..., or *Like all spinsters she* ..., or *Only a duchess could have.* ... These statements are not apodeictic because of some actual law of which the narrator reminds his readers, they are apodeictic and self-sufficient because a specific fact is inserted into a generalizing syntagm—without, however, producing a designation for the general category: the same word points now to a class, now to a token of that class.

For instance, in the Balzacian phrase *Like all spinsters she* ..., placing *she* into the class of spinsters is a given that does not affect or limit the unfolding of a narrative sequence in which many characters may fit, but the unfolding of the diegetic derivation will select motivations among the possibilities offered by the class to which this particular character belongs. Hence transformations generate a story whose end product still refers unchangingly to the input of the given: *This spinster, being a spinster, acted like one*, or *This spinster, despite being a spinster, acted quite unlike one.* How can the reader deny the truth of a predication without content, a sign without referent, a mere index of didacticism? So incontrovertible is this device that it even displaces or preempts those descriptive details that are supposed to be verifiable, the litmus test of reality. Once again, Balzac is full of such statements: *He made one of those gestures that, to the experienced observer, reveal,* etc. The gesture is not described; the knowing but equally unspecified observer stands only for the stereotype contrasting a major significance and a minor signal (as in the phrase *tell-tale glance*). What we have is not even a sign standing for a significance, but a sign standing for a sign. The entailment that the gesture hypothesizes is thus true.

To be sure, these instances are extreme ones, but extreme cases are not exceptions; they are, rather, hyperbolic variables in a paradigm of comparable types or categories. Far be it from me to suggest that verisimilitude in fiction is always independent of readers' assumptions about reality, of their pragmatic knowledge, of their experience of people or their familiarity with the ways of the world. I am saying only that such assumptions and pragmatic experience vary widely, that ideological changes color reality with many hues, and that a narrative must contain features that are self-verifiable and therefore resistant to the vagaries of reference. These features are the same structural identity of sememes and narrative units that we have examined, the same tautological, circular derivations, but instead of referring to images or indices of verifiability in the abstract, they parallel in language the cognitive processes we use in everyday life.

Such is the case with those passages in a narrative that strike us by their justness, keen perception of behavior, neat sense of psychological observation. That these powers of observation are actually rooted in structures, that they are tautological and therefore pseudo-transformations, can be readily seen in this scene from one of Henry James's early novels, *Washington Square* (1880). In that Jamesian version of *Eugénie Grandet,* which takes place, however, among a more genteel class of people, a lonely, vulnerable girl, the only daughter of a wealthy physician, is being courted, or rather her father's money is being courted, by an elegant, seductive, sexy, and utterly worthless suitor. The father has seen through him, shown him the door, and taken his romantic, naive child on a European grand tour, the usual cure a hundred years ago for the rash infatuations of gullible scions or starry-eyed heiresses. As soon as they are back, the daughter again meets with her persistent lover. Her foolish, meddling aunt tells her how she secretly abetted the seducer's schemes and regularly received him in her father's townhouse:

> "He used to sit in your father's study" said Mrs. Penniman, with a little laugh.
> Catherine was silent a moment. This idea was disagreeable to her, and she was reminded again, with pain, of her aunt's secretive habits. Morris, the reader may be informed, had had the tact not to tell her that he sat in her father's study. He had known her but for a few months, and her aunt had known her for fifteen years; and yet he would not have made the mistake of thinking that Catherine would see the joke of the thing. "I am sorry you made him go into father's room," she said, after a while.
> "I didn't send him; he went himself. He liked to look at the books, and at all those things in the glass cases. He knows all about them; he knows all about everything."
> Catherine was silent again.[3]

Readers will of course feel the impropriety of the man's conduct almost as keenly as Catherine herself does. They will perceive him as crafty in a way that is even worse than the aunt's "innocent falsity" (ibid., 120). Readers will also recognize the justness of the trait, how sharply it brings out the man's base designs and how typical they are of a Lothario. But why do we concur? What inspires this sense of the revealingly true detail?

No doubt, it may be that the episode rings true because

the text itself explicitly comments on the man's behavior and also because of the irony ("He would not have made the mistake of thinking that Catherine would see the joke of the thing"). One might think, however, that we would not readily accept the narrator's interpretation or the irony about Morris's tact if experience had not taught us that some people behave that way and what to expect from them. But what of the reader who has led a sheltered life? Language still provides him with stereotyped stories about this type of person: there is, in the lexicon of the sociolect, a collection of set portraits for the genus scoundrel, class of money hunters, species of dowry snatchers. Even if we assume that some gullible readers are also innocent of clichés, innocent in general, or just plain stupid, the narrative palliates their simplemindedness with a grammatical framework engineered to ensure proper interpretation.

Morris Townsend, James's fortune hunter, has sat in the father's study, looked at his books and at his art collection. The implication is clear that, consciously or not, he was playing at displacing the father, first by coveting objects that are the father's metonyms, books representing his interests, prized possessions, his pleasures. Thus the hermit crab appropriates another mollusk's shell, thus the cuckoo settles in another bird's nest. The text first outlines a spatial frame for a character, second, substitutes the frame for its occupant, and, third, inserts a new occupant into that frame. This is the structure here, within which substitution is a symbolic act. This structure can serve as a model instantly recognizable anywhere. Better still, it remains recognizable even if we have never seen the model before, because the grammatical frame is clearly a transform of the first occupant by expansion from one word or name into a periphrastic sequence of metonyms, and because the lexicon that defines the intruder, in fitting that periphrastic frame, represents a transformation that one word will summarize: the word *parasite*. To recognize the truth of this, neither experience nor previous readings are needed, only linguistic competence: truth is nothing but a linguistic perception. Abuse or swindling is not stated; if it were, we might have a chance to disagree with the narrator's judgment or to excuse the character for some personal reason or arbitrary preference.

The well-defined frame we have in the James example, and the ease of substitution it affords, is a linguistic given developed, as it were, from a program already implicit in the character of the father, that is, in the *father* sememe.

Models generating the diegesis are by no means limited to isolated sememes. There can be no representation of reality without involving a sequence of sememes, each producing in turn its own descriptive system or those components of it that are relevant in context. At this point, semiosis intervenes and changes the whole sequence of those interrelated systems into as many conventional codes for the telling of another story.

This sweeping change is accomplished by the interpretant. As C. S. Peirce, the father of semiotics, defines it, the interpretant is the idea to which the relationship of sign to object gives rise; that is, it is yet another sign that in turn cannot be interpreted without our finding its object sign and involving an interpretant mediating between the first interpretant and that object. As the narrative unfolds, the successive signs all engender such interrelationships, and if constants occur—if, for instance, successive signs have similar interpretants—the continuous semiosis regulating interpretation will become a unidirectional transformation. Whatever the story says will then stand for something else. The successive meanings ticked off by the verbal sequence will merge into one significance. Whatever the text represents, whatever its mimesis reflects, will, by the agency of cumulative semiosis, be changed into a series of similarly modified representations. Thus mimesis—based on verisimilitude, differences, and successivity—gives way to representation—based on repetition and equivalences adhering to one single rule. The resulting combination of tautology and circularity (the sum total being the equivalent of the original given) is now perceived as a permanent, unchanging symbolic Truth.

The translation of the father into his things can be found on a wider scale, extending to the whole stage on which the narrative describes a situation and plays out a scene: semiosis then metamorphoses that description into a code for the actor's feelings. Suppose a female protagonist falls in love with a man, although unconsciously. Suppose further that she is surrounded with metonyms of the object of her love. The mimesis of this setting is tantamount to a periphrasis of that object. The protagonist's desire being then translated into a projection onto the libidinal object, semiosis will compel readers to interpret its mimesis as a code for the subject's craving. Diegesis will be like a geometry, a grammar shifting the focus from an apparent reality to a cathexis or narcissistic transference onto it. To be sure, the mimesis is lexical, but its words will be downgraded to having the function of indices: they will merely indicate the direction pointed to by the protagonist's desire.

In *Pride and Prejudice,* for instance, the female protagonist visits a country estate in the absence of its owner, who wants to marry her and whose offer she has spurned. She admires the tasteful layout of the grounds, the elegant splendor of the manor house. The reader is led to believe that he is looking at things through her eyes, whereas in fact he is made to witness the objectifying of her libido. Jane Austen narrates the birth of love, and her love story is couched in terms of landscaping and interior decorating. Moreover, the sensory denotations of the landscape and furniture lexicon are canceled out, so that only the positive marking remains as a hermeneutic guideline: we understand Elizabeth Bennett. This particular description provides the reader with sketches of ideal but necessary landscape components: hills and valleys, rivers and forests. It is complete but nondescript, like an encyclopedia entry under *landscape* or *topography.*

This system of locales, however, only serves as an interesting and even prevalorized syntactic grid conferring functions to lexical units, each of which is structured as a predication. In each of these units, subject and predicate are like two slots of the same frame. One slot is filled with a descriptive word pertaining to the lexicon of the picturesque, a word the perception of which will satisfy readers that the text is about sensory perception, about experiencing sightseeing—a walk in a park or visit to a country seat of the British aristocracy. The other slot is filled with a word from the discourse of desire. If that slot is filled with a noun, the other one takes a descriptive adjective appropriate for a picturesque frame or context. If the slot for desire is filled with an adjective, the descriptive slot is filled with a noun such as *tree, valley, hill,* and so on. But the point is that the descriptive lexicon is varied, multiple, and detailed, whereas the libidinal lexicon, with its repetitive and synonymic nouns and adjectives, enacts the scene of desire either by dint of repetition, by dint of synonyms, or by exhausting the supply of metonyms of whatever is desired:

> The park was very large, and contained great variety of ground. They entered it in one of its lowest points, and drove for some time through a beautiful wood, stretching over a wide extent.
>
> Elizabeth's mind was too full for conversation, but she saw and admired every remarkable spot and point of view. They gradually ascended for half a mile, and then found themselves at the top of a considerable eminence, where the wood ceased, and the eye was instantly caught by Pemberley House, situated on the

opposite side of a valley, into which the road with some abruptness wound. It was a large, handsome, stone building, standing
well on rising ground, and backed by a ridge of high woody
hills;—and in front, a stream of some natural importance was
swelled into greater, but without any artificial appearance. Its
banks were neither formal, nor falsely adorned. Elizabeth was
delighted. She had never seen a place for which nature had done
more, or where natural beauty had been so little counteracted by
an awkward taste.[4]

Strictly speaking, we see nothing beyond the barest components: obviously, these are props for repeating verbs of
praise and adjectives such as *large, beautiful,* and *handsome*
that are no mimesis but all semiosis, eliciting as they do from
the successive sign-object relations one single interpretant:
the silhouette of the owner as a man worthy of Elizabeth's
love.

The visitors are received in the house, and we get more of
the same, this time in interior decorating code:

the dining-parlour ... was a large, well-proportioned room,
handsomely fitted up. Elizabeth, after slightly surveying it, went
to a window to enjoy its prospect. The hill, crowned with wood,
from which they had descended, receiving increased abruptness
from the distance, was a beautiful object. Every disposition of
the ground was good; and she looked on the whole scene, the
river, the trees scattered on its banks, and the winding of the valley, as far as she could trace it, with delight. As they passed into
other rooms, these objects were taking different positions; but
from every window there were beauties to be seen. The rooms
were lofty and handsome, and their furniture suitable to the fortune of their proprietor; but Elizabeth saw, with admiration of
his taste, that it was neither gaudy nor uselessly fine; with less of
splendor, and more real elegance, than the furniture of Rosings.
(Ibid., 167)

We may think that the one specific notation about changing perspectives signals a return to the picturesque, to objective mimesis. Far from it: this was a standard requirement for tasteful buildings, and the description of these varied vantage points therefore expands the word *beautiful* into a sentence once again.

Such a saturation is the triumph of semiosis over mimesis: it works very much like the grammars of allegorical emblems in Baroque poetry. In such interpretation-dictating representations, the body, if the allegory consists of a personification, is only a pretext for repeating the personified concept. The adjectives modifying the nouns of the limbs of the body or the garments adorning them may seem to characterize them separately, but adjectivation exhibits consistent features that in fact correspond to the allegorized idea rather than to its physical embodiment. Adjectives form a repetitive series saturating the character's anatomy with tags that bear the emblematic message.

In order to demonstrate that verisimilitude does not stop at the mimesis and that, instead, the ultimate truth of the narrative depends on semiosis, on saturating the mimesis with repetitive modifiers, let us compare the visit to Pemberley to the story of a hunting party's arrival in what one of the hunters calls "a very ugly country." The place is Scotland, the time of year grouse-shooting season. The novel is Anthony Trollope's *The Duke's Children:*

> the country through which they had passed for the last twenty miles had been not only bleak and barren, but uninteresting and ugly. It was all rough open moorland, never rising into mountains, and graced by no running streams, by no forest scenery, almost by no foliage.[5]

These few lines do no more than repeat the initial adjectives, *bleak and barren,* but since in language you cannot describe the absence or lack of something without naming that something, the descriptive system of the word *landscape* has to be actualized, hence a derivation producing the same landscape as at Austen's Pemberley. This would be paradoxical or even ludicrous if truth directly stemmed from a likeness of reality. It appears, however, perfectly logical and efficacious when we recognize that the generation of such a narrative begins with a lexical given selected in terms of whatever situation, events, or characterization demands (in most, if not all, cases, in terms of the telos). The second step consists in objectifying and thus motivating the narrative derived from that given by saturating the descriptive with variants of a seme of the given or with markings reflecting the given's significance. For this purpose the narrative has at its disposal descriptive frames that are phrasal amplifications of the lexical given, periphrases of the given whose components can be used to harp upon the proairetic selection of the given's interpretation. This time the landscape must be negative: each stereotyped component of the periphrasis, each detail is accordingly modified by a *no* (*no streams, no forest, no foliage*) that cancels it. As we go on, it is like a ghost image of Darcy's estate that rises from the ground, but systematically negativized rather than merely negated:

> The lodge itself did indeed stand close upon a little river, and was reached by a bridge that crossed it; but there was nothing pretty either in the river or the bridge. It was a placid black little streamlet, which in that portion of its course was hurried by no steepness, had no broken rocks in its bed, no trees on its low banks, and played none of those gambols which make running water beautiful. The bridge was a simple low construction with a low parapet, the house itself was as ugly as a house could be, white, of two stories, with the door in the middle and windows on each side, with a slate roof and without a tree near it.
>
> (Ibid.)

The cathexis is, however, in this case negative only for human beings, which is to say that it is positive for their animal counterparts and that what looks barren to the hunter looks like paradise to the birds. The owner of the hunting lodge, a no-nonsense sportsman, gives the key to significance:

> "Ugly, do you call it?"
> "Infernally ugly," said Lord Gerald.
> "What did you expect to find? A big hotel, and a lot of cockneys? If you come after grouse, you must come to what the grouse thinks pretty."
>
> (Ibid.)

There is no functional difference between the illegitimate occupation of the study in the townhouse of *Washington Square*, the visit to Pemberley, and the sportsmen's arrival at the shooting grounds in Trollope. Townsend in the father's room, Elizabeth in Darcy's place, and men in birds' country are there because of their desires, inserting their respective subjects into the objects of that desire, investing these objects with their libido. The most sketchy verisimilitude therefore characterizes the description of the objects, because their sole function is to provide a frame within which the pervasive statement of desire can be expressed repeatedly. The only point of the representation of reality is to charge it with the value it has for the character. The verisimilar story unfolds only as a vehicle for valorization, being in itself a pretext, a sort of make-believe. Truth is performative and therefore not to be denied or ignored: again, no reader can go through these episodes without enacting the obsessive variation on a state of mind. Hence the characterization and the power of psychological fixation, the necessity resulting from a uniform coloring of shapes, places, and actors by the protagonist's gaze.

Furthermore, the development of the tautology through

variables in the description of space and time is also the textual generator, the agency for the production of narrative. The story has to unfold from place to place, from detail to detail, along the time dimension for those places, details, and moments to become the members of a paradigm of synonyms, all of which are variants mirroring the permanent, context-free, and, therefore, true picture of a mental state.

Repetition involves both the subject and the object. As for the former, repetition is at once the index of the subject's behavior towards the object and therefore a narrative given, and also the grammatical frame for the story's progression (here, the subject's walk through the landscape). Similarly, as far as the object is concerned, repetition indicates that a person, in the Austen example the character of the spurned suitor, is now translated into things, which therefore become monuments of his taste, or, more technically, signs referring to his mental features, all positively marked. Since the positive marker appears in a predication that defines the subject as perceiving these qualities, repetition both transforms the object into an object of desire and proposes new clues for our interpretation of the subject: hence, on the reader's part, the experience of being ahead of the character who plays subject, the feeling that they know more about her than she does herself. This experience is, of course, a sign of truth conquered or unearthed from appearances and also a sign that has a narrative function. Repetition, therefore, is both the technical means for the narrative to progress (here through the description of a landscape, the walk through that landscape being a symbolic review of one character's thoughts about another) and for truth to be revealed.

Without speculating about when a repetition becomes perceptible, as in those philosophical arguments on how many strands have to be plucked before a head of hair becomes a balding pate, it is safe to say that saying the same thing twice does not go beyond a stylistic variation or a mild sign of insistence and that repetition does not become a trope before the third time. If this is so, then I propose to find my test for this interpretation of narrative truth as unchanging iteration within a changing story in Lewis Carroll's *Hunting of the Snark* (Fit 1, l. 8) in the Bellman's injunction to his crew: *What I tell you three times is true.*[6]

In all instances that have been examined so far, fictional truth has been produced by make-believe transformations and structures interposed between textual verisimilitude and reality, but the narrative always seems to try to veil the gap between factuality and verisimilitude. Indeed, the drift of most of narratology today is to understand the role of discourse as both an implementation of narrative structures and the construction of a network of causes, of explanations (mostly psychological) to give the mechanical derivation of the narrative the legitimacy, or authority, of mimesis. My discussion of the paradoxical blend of fiction and truth suggests, on the contrary, that narrative verisimilitude tends to flaunt rather than mask its fictitious nature.

Moreover, there is in fiction a type of derivation in which the diegesis is generated from words or phrases foreign to the convention of verisimilitude that is peculiar to the story. These generators may belong to the narrator's discourse, or to a tropology inconsistent with the mimesis (a metaphor, for example, for which no character could be responsible or that is at variance with the values connoted or the aims denoted by the situation). Such derivations therefore display fictionality while producing verisimilar sequences. More significantly still, these sequences develop into subtexts that mirror the whole of the text in which they are embedded and therefore facilitate the text's interpretation.

The following example of such a subtext is from *The Egoist* (1879) by Meredith, a rare case of a feminist novel by a male writer, a tale of rejection with the usual roles happily reversed: an unsufferably blind sexist—a selfish, vain, and wealthy member of the British landed aristocracy—selects a spirited young woman as his bride and the mother of his heirs-to-be. Social and family pressure would seem to have condemned her to matrimonial enslavement. The heroine, however, rebels and jilts him. The subtext extends through almost five hundred of the novel's six hundred pages, but it is sparsely spread over a dozen passages. Readers nevertheless quickly learn to recognize such passages as being equivalent to one another, and to remember all the preceding variants each time a new one is found. A metaphorical characterization of Clara as a piece of elegant and frail Dresden china begets successive episodes in which actual pieces of china, wedding presents, symbolize the marital prison for which she seems destined. The fact that they get broken or that she refuses them announces her rebellion and subsequent freedom. The subtext is thus so central to the plot that it belongs to the *mise en abyme* category; it is a mini-narrative encapsulating the narrative that contains it, a specularity, a mirroring of text by subtext reminiscent of the Romantic conceit of the oak tree potential within the acorn.

The given that initiates this subtext is an inspired witticism with which the egoist's confidante pinpoints the elusiveness of his fiancée, an "elfishness, tricksiness, freakishness"[7] suggesting that she may bolt. This "wild card" in her character is balanced, to some extent, by her slim figure and her British complexion (she looks like a biscuit statuette) that evince elegance and frailty. Cleverly juxtaposing the two facets, the confidante pronounces her to be a "dainty rogue in porcelain" (ibid., 75). This given, an epigram in the text, seems to serve as an epigraph to the subtext.

Needless to say, Sir Willoughby's reading of Clara produces an entirely different, and mistaken, interpretation, his "ideal of a waxwork sex" (ibid., chap. 34, 415), modeled on the sociolect's hermeneutic template of Woman as submissive wife and passive mother: to him Clara is "essentially feminine, in other words, a parasite and chalice" (ibid., chap. 5, 78). *Waxwork sex* betrays one of men's favorite delusions, that women are easily shaped and impressed (like wax) under Pygmalion's thumb. As for *parasite*, it means that woman plays ivy to man's tree, and *chalice* is a pompous sacralization veiling the blunt reduction of woman to a vase or grail for man's seed.

The incompatibility of the two readings now develops into the subtext proper through a new variant, the mimesis of Sir Willoughby's querulous response to *dainty rogue:*

> "She is a charming young woman, only she is one of that sort."
> "Of what sort?" Sir Willoughby asked, impatiently.
> "Rogues in porcelain."
> "I am persuaded I shall never comprehend it."
> "I cannot help you one bit further."
> "The word rogue!"
> "It was dainty rogue."
> "Brittle, would you say?"
> "I am quite unable to say."
> "An innocent naughtiness?"
> "Prettily molded in a delicate substance."
> "You are thinking of some piece of Dresden . . . "
> "I dare say."
> "Artificial?"
> "You would not have her natural?"
>
> (Ibid., 78–79)

Each term thus examined and questioned becomes, in turn, the generator of narrative developments: *brittle,* for instance, starts a derivation from the negative side of *dainty* applied to a semanalysis of *porcelain.* The positive side of *dainty* continues to protect Clara against the pejorative connotations of *rogue*. Thus valorized, the terms will now dictate the narrative, but they do so through a succession of events and situations. Each of these, whether dynamic concatenation or static tableau, will be none other than a description amplifying each of the definitions of the original terms. As a result, the descriptions become a lexicon organized by the diegetic syntax, but that syntax is itself generated by the grammar of the first description—one that acquires its creative power from its imagistic, disconcerting conspicuousness. Description begets narrative; in fact, narrative cannot come into being without description.

The *porcelain* subtext, being metaphoric in origin, develops into events that partake of the substance "porcelain" as incidents and of the metaphoric acceptation of the word *porcelain* as symbol. Thus, Clara, driven to flight by Sir Willoughby's insistence upon an early wedding, is on her way to the railroad station all by herself, a very rash and roguish demeanor in the context of Victorian propriety. She is almost run over on the road, and, in the resulting confusion, the carriage bringing the best man to the nuptials is upset. His wedding present breaks into pieces: it was, as one might guess, a magnificent china vase. The confidante dutifully appears in order to deliver her commentary, which translates meaning as detail into significance as sign: "Well, now, the gift can be shared, if you're either of you for a division" (ibid., chap. 17, 214). In legal terminology, *division* refers to a marriage contract. Of course, everyday usage and the character's irony prompt a tempting second interpretation that underscores the broken vase's announcement of an impending parting of the ways. This second reading is confirmed narratively: "In the crash of the carriage-wheels [Sir Willoughby] heard, 'At any rate there was a rogue in that porcelain'" (ibid.). (This is a sentence in which *crash* refers to the noise of wheels on gravel but also echoes the symbolic accident, whereby the adjective *brittle,* Willoughby's negative descriptive interpretation of *dainty* a hundred fifty pages earlier, is now changed into a narration realizing of what had previously appeared to be a premonition.)

Later, Clara refuses to discuss the wedding presents with a lady who is planning to offer her a china dinner service. Evidently Clara cannot possibly know that an observer has been identifying her with porcelain. Only the reader can connect the two threads. Finally, the engagement is broken. Wan and exhausted by the crisis she has gone through, Clara now looks "like a bit of china that wants dusting" (ibid., chap. 46, 553). This comparison serves as a clausula for the subtext, as though the erasure of the given were completed by changing *dainty,* the adjective describing her in the incipit, into *dusty.*

The signs that function as indices pointing to fictionality are, I think, quite visible, so much so, in fact, as to survive any lapse of attention on the part of the reader. First of all, the very consistency of the symbolic avatars of porcelain, in whatever form objects made of that material appear, is, as the phrase goes, too good to be true. And so, for that matter, is the coincidence that upsets the best man's carriage to avoid running Clara over, breaking his wedding present and thus saving her twice, both now and in the future, actually and figuratively. The showman shows his hand. Evidently, such obviousness is designed to represent the artist and his artifice even more clearly than would conventional authorial intrusions.

Second, the *china* derivation crosses the logical frontiers separating characters, at the expense of their respective integrity. This derivation flouts verisimilitude, blurring the borders between sets of circumstances that should remain distinct, painting them, as it were, with the same (porcelain) glaze. Despite the variety of voices and the changing situations and successive events, there seems to be a single discourse, the narrator's, spoken through his characters, regardless of their different and sometimes contrary states of mind. The same images flow from Sir Willoughby's *chalice* to his confidante's *porcelain*, and, as I have noted, they even intrude into Clara's psyche, although she should be the last to know how others view her. Poured from different vases, these metaphors all end up in the same heap of broken crockery. Every characterization, every localization, every telling difference is momentarily blanketed over by one obsessive trope.

What now of the truth, after this challenge to the accepted, believable ways of telling a story? To be sure, the subtext does some credit to Meredith's powers of observation: *chalice* has the pomposity we expect from Sir Willoughby, and *dainty rogue* sounds like something a woman of the world would say. Any fledgling writer, however, could rise to this minor realism; the depiction of Clara disliking whatever reminds her of her predicament is not beyond the ken of a first semester's creative writing class. The real truth lies elsewhere, in the transformation that makes a ceramic lexicon into a diegetic code for a significant change at the narrative level. Any narrative recounts the progress or the decay of a situational given. Here, the china code translates the story of a decaying situation into images that are overdetermined equally by two readings of the character enacting the paradoxical given of roguish delicacy. The first of these readings is correct, whereas the second is the antithesis of the first. This is merely another way of repeating and confirming the former. For each component or variant in the sequence of events, synonyms or metonyms of *china* repeat its figurative message. For each incident, the telling circumstances (i.e., breakage) actualize essential semes of the initial sememes. Furthermore, for each successive sign in the narrative, the relation of sign to object is regulated by the same interpretant; each time, the sign points not to its object but to the shift from *breakable* to *breaking off*. In other words, the diegetic sequence that organizes the jilt story is primarily the verbal frame for a paradigm of repetitive symbols. The syntax is narrative, but the lexicon it seems to distribute in time and space is lyric, a bundle of symbols divided into two sets, one positive, the other negative—delicate Dresden, dusty china.

These symbols thus translate into poetic discourse, within the narrower compass of the subtext, the significance that requires the full length of the novel to develop into narrative discourse. This mirroring of the whole into one of its parts, this key to the text's way of making its point, is, in its turn, made apparent in the most blatant sign of fictionality. Sir Willoughby's first name is remarkable in itself since it sounds so much like the first names one expects of the gentry. It must evoke the cognomen of an ancient lineage since it so obviously differs from the average baptismal name. The singularity of it is bound to facilitate an intertextual connection with another Willoughby, another conceited male persecutor of defenseless young women: the heroine's offensive suitor in Fanny Burney's *Evelina*. Furthermore, Fanny Burney's character provides Jane Austen's readers with the intertext that helps them unmask *her* John Willoughby's selfishness long before Marianne sees through him in *Sense and Sensibility. Willoughby*, therefore, is already a conventional tag for Meredith's readers. The fictional nature of the tag, however, does not alter the truth of the type or types it designates (the insensitive male, jilting or jilted). In any case, the tag sets off more visibly *Patterne, our* Sir Willoughby's patronymic, the referential sign that distinguishes him from his functional analogues in Burney and Austen. With such visibility, it will not take long for Meredith's readers to realize that Sir *Willoughby Patterne* is, in fact, a syllepsis for *willow pattern*, a pattern for chinaware that is still popular. The reader may long resist the evidence, because the artifice is so outrageous. Yet this formal excess, this elusive rejection of verisimilitude, completes the imagistic grammar and adds the final logical touch to what amounts to an overall transformation from sociolect to idiolect. Against all likelihood and yet with perfect logic, the characters and their interaction are translated into a *china* code—a sign system equally apt, as we have seen, for betrothal and betrayal.

The subtext as a whole is a deixis of truth for yet another reason, the most important one perhaps and the one that has the widest applicability, since it is a function rather than the objects whose relationships this function regulates. It is a geometry of those relationships, a form rather than a content. The reason is that the subtext always constitutes a second reading of what the text surrounding it is about, a poetic or humorous metalanguage of the narrative. The subtext thus actualizes the relationship of referentiality. Whether it metonymically develops a specific aspect of the story in which it is embedded or whether it substitutes a metaphor for it, the subtext is like an illustration or an example isolating and emphasizing a moment of the story. The main story is therefore presupposed to be true. There is no need for any further confirmation or objective correlative of that truth: the referential gesture pointing to the text amounts to the surmise that whatever the text narrates is either anterior or exterior to the subtextual sign system and therefore equivalent to an authority for whatever the subtext tells us. It is in fact equivalent to a reality that the subtext represents a second time in a different way. Relative to the subtextual gloss on the narrative or developing a moment, an event, or a character in it, that narrative has assumed the function of a referent. The narrative is to the subtext as an object is to its sign.

Two

Fictionality Declared

Signs pointing to the fictionality of fiction are many and well known. The list is extensive: authors' intrusions; narrators' intrusions; multiple narrators; humorous narrative that acts as a representation of the author or of a narrator or that suggests an outsider's viewpoint without fully intruding; meta-language glossing narrative language; generic markers in the titles and subtitles, in prefaces, and in postfaces; emblematic names for characters and places; incompatibilities between narrative voice and viewpoint and characters' voices and viewpoints; incompatibilities between viewpoint and verisimilitude, especially omniscient narrative; signs modifying the narrative's pace and altering the sequence of events (backtracking and anticipation, significant gaps, prolepsis, and analepsis); mimetic excesses, such as unlikely recordings of unimportant speech or thought (unimportant but suggestive of actual happenings, of a live presence, creating atmosphere or characterizing persons); and, finally, diegetic overkill, such as the representation of ostensibly insignificant details, the very insignificance of which is significant in a story as a feature of realism. Narratology seems to have neglected the constant coincidence between textual features declaring the fictionality of a story and a reassertion of the truth of that story.

There is a touching, if somewhat ridiculous, scene in *Middlemarch* in which Eliot describes the persistently blind love of Dorothea, that symbol of hopeless naiveté, for her dried-up scholar of a husband:

> With all her yearning to know what was afar from her and to be widely benignant, she had ardour enough for what was near, to have kissed Mr. Casaubon's coat-sleeve, or to have caressed his shoe-latchet, if he would have made any other sign of acceptance than pronouncing her, with his unfailing propriety, to be a most affectionate and truly feminine nature, indicating at the same time by politely reaching a chair for her that he regarded these manifestations as rather crude and startling.[1]

Kissing the hem of a priest's robes is not an unusual gesture of worship, and John the Baptist considered himself unworthy of untying Jesus's sandals according to all four Gospels. But the effect of these traditional gestures applied to modern articles of clothing is of course comical, and this comicality suggests a parody of reality rather than a representation of it. The reader may gloss over this first impression by assuming that Dorothea, in her effusive élan, might have caught her husband's coat sleeve at the very moment he was withdrawing his hand from her. This explanation, however, becomes untenable at the appearance of the shoe-latchet, the more so because *shoe-latchet* somehow makes things worse than just *shoe* by preventing us from dismissing it as figurative. We cannot suppose that she is actually kissing or caressing Casaubon's feet, which would be a Magdalen cliché. Fetishism, or at least female fetishism, would be incredible in a nineteenth-century marital relationship and certainly in a literary representation thereof. The implausible exaggeration of the gesture, the metonymic reduction of the character to his clothes, reification itself being an effective farcical device, the substitution of things for whatever humanity is left in Casaubon and the playful neotestamentary allusion (for Mark 1:7, Luke 3:16, and John 1:27 are unanimous in making the Baptist specify *shoe's latchet*)—all this clearly interposes between the scene and us, its spectators, the screen of the author's irony. It indicates a deliberate encoding of intention, an intrusion tantamount to the public exposure of a private intercourse too embarrassing, if accurately represented, to be mentioned. At the same time, however, the improbably wildness of Dorothea's reaching out is true to form, since she has defined herself as an embodiment of imprudent impulse from the first pages of the novel. Likewise, Mr. Casaubon's hasty retreat behind a proffered chair may be a caricature, but, given the context, it is a likely thing to do for anyone thus sexually confronted.

On the one hand, therefore, the farcical exaggeration, the biblical reference, and the narrator's stated viewpoint bespeak artifice and focus on the presence and, nearly, the participation of that narrator in the scene. These are signs of fictionality. On the other hand, the unlikely scene is true, even though it is so obviously contrived that verisimilitude is suspended.

Critics, in general, and narratologists, in particular, react to these contradictory signals sent to them by the text by trying to demonstrate that the narrative makes up for the loss of verisimilitude, that for each fictional index there is a compensatory increase of narrative motivation.

In *Barchester Towers,* a moment of suspense occurs when

a classical comedy of errors delays the awaited mutual admission of love.

> As she spoke she with difficulty restrained her tears—but she did restrain them. Had she given way and sobbed aloud, as in such cases a woman should do, he would have melted at once, implored her pardon, perhaps knelt at her feet and declared his love. Everything would have been explained, and Eleanor would have gone back to Barchester with a contented mind. How easily would she have forgiven and forgotten the archdeacon's suspicions had she but heard the whole truth from Mr. Arabin. But then where would have been my novel? She did not cry, and Mr. Arabin did not melt.[2]

Meir Sternberg, in his 1983 essay on "Mimesis and Motivation," comments that "Trollope's display of artifice is still coupled with a quasi-mimetic justification on psychological and situational grounds—after all, it *is* a fact that she did not cry or he melt."[3]

What is actually taking place here, it seems to me, is not a mimetic compensation correcting fictionality but an increase of the latter. The whole paragraph is but a transformation of the author's aside ("where would have been my novel"), its text having become the periphrastic equivalent of that aside. The sentence, "Had she given way . . . as in such cases a woman should do, he would have," etc., spells out the options of fictionality, especially the reference to ideological stereotypes straight out of the sociolect (*as a woman should do*). By proposing, side by side, one sequence of events in the subjunctive mood and one in the indicative, one potential and one actualized story, the text in fact represents proairesis itself, the author's program of options and the generic differences to be expected from the choice; what we have, in short, is a commentary about a narrative rule. Hence two truths are stated—a general truth, that things do not always turn out to be easy or positive, and an esthetic truth about how a novel can be enjoyed, depending on whether a short or a long narrative itinerary is chosen. All of this is achieved by replacing mimetic with metalinguistic discourse.

Signs of fictionality in a text are not veiled or blunted or compensated for by corrective verisimilitude that suspends disbelief; rather, it is these very signs that point to a truth invulnerable to the deficiencies of mimesis or to the reader's resistance to it. They do so by suspending belief, by radically displacing verisimilitude.

Emblematic names, that is to say, patronymics with a meaning related to the part played by their bearers in a story, are especially blatant indices of fictionality. Critics tend to see them as the most obvious hindrance to verisimilitude. It is true enough that when Trollope calls a physician *Dr. Fillgrave*, names the partners of a law firm *Slow and Bideawhile*, or dubs a breechmaker *Mr. Neefit*, removing the initial "K" as the only concession to appearances, readers know precisely what to make of it. They recognize in the first an allusion to a traditional satire of medicine's limitations, they understand the allusion to the habitual procrastination of the legal system, and they also realize, however laughingly, that a tailor specializing in riding breeches must make sure they come down nicely to the knee. Readers also find this too good to be true, and yet they play along, more or less readily. The sociolect has a special place for telltale family names or ones that have influenced a man's choice of career.

This mythology is indeed the point of reference for a novel to develop a life in accordance with what's in a name: in Balzac's *Illusions Perdues* the name of the protagonist, Séchard, which more or less means *dried up*, is, according to the narrator, the reason he turned into a drunkard. At the man's first appearance, we are told that "bound by the laws of etymology to be a dry subject, he suffered from an inextinguishable thirst."⁴ A portrayal follows, rereading this program into the stigmata of heavy drinking on his face. When this tautological paradigm is exhausted (we know it is when the paradigm, having run out of synonyms, finds its variants through puns or quotations—in short, outside the sociolect), the other option for derivations, the oxymoric one, is set in motion with a tale of how clever Séchard is despite his drunkenness. Even the shrewdness of the businessman in him is served by his stultified appearance: the people he deals with do not realize how sharp his mind remains despite the fumes of alcohol. Again, Balzac, introducing the character who gives his name to another novel, Z. *Marcas*, explains his unhappy fate in one of those apodeictic statements that, as I have noted, are uncontrovertible because of their generality and because they look axiomatic:

> Between the events of a life and people's names, there exist secret and inexplicable concordances or visible disparities that astonish . . . Perhaps we should some day return to occult sciences. Would you not say that the Z [of his first name] looks as if something had twisted its development? Does it not represent the chance and fantastic zigzagging of a tormented life?⁵

The rest of the novel tells of the character's ups and downs, and ends with his failure. It is as if the overdetermined motivations that make for verisimilitude had been unfolding backwards to end at the starting point of the title, the fated name whose ominous form indeed is like a visible image of the plot's telos: visible, and therefore a guideline for the proper interpretation of events as indicating the hand of fate, and vindicating the name.

These two examples are impure, so to speak, and of dubious value for my demonstration, because they use popular wisdom as a reference, a mimetic factor rather than narrative motivation. But in all pure cases, a derivation from the name's meaning retroactively verifies and motivates that meaning; the story becomes a follow-up or a consequence of that semantic given, and the diegesis is derived from its descriptive and narrative transformations. Both Trollope's suffragette Baroness Banman and Virginia Woolf's Miss Kilman speak and act out a totalitarian feminism, and Dickens's Barnacle family is indeed encrusted on the ship of state.

However, not every emblematic name is parodic. The norm is that they designate a character trait, a behavior, an occupation, or even a trade through a name, an adjective, or a short phrase the components of which are linked together like the syllables of one word. These designations are literal, metaphorical, or metonymic. There is no way that a long-established family name might have been acquired by virtue of one of those traits. The coincidence, therefore, annihilates verisimilitude.

The character, however, acts as if the name, instead of being bequeathed to him, had been chosen as a tag for his way of life or his temperament. He embodies what the tag says. The emblematic name posits a truth, because it designates not a person but a type. The character behind that tag, a character whose characteristics are indeed generated by the corresponding definition, denotative or connotative, is thus exemplary. For truth to be generated, the meaningless, and therefore, verisimilar, family name had to become meaningful; thus, the name functions like a syllepsis. As a name, it represses its meaning, and, conversely, as the noun it could have been, now repressed by grammar and spelling (the initial is capitalized), it generates a text consistent with its content or symbolism.

The text thus proceeds by verifying the kind of action expected of the type through a convincing, that is to say, tautological, story. Verisimilitude canceled out by the name is recreated by the story in which that name defines not an actor but a kind of actor, and for which it sketches a program.

In Trollope's *The Three Clerks,* in which the protagonist is tried for embezzlement, there rises a powerful, loud, over-bearing barrister by the name of Chaffanbrass. Despite the name and its aptness, he is no mere caricature, as are the leading counsel who processes paperwork and plans defense strategies, Mr. Gitemthruet, and that aspiring barrister, Mr. Younglad. The difference is that the last two, being bit players to make the picture of the defense staff complete, bear names that remain undeveloped into textual veridiction, whereas Mr. Chaffanbrass generates four tautological diegetic derivations and one oxymoric one. After a brief review of his strong suit (he specializes in getting patent culprits off the hook), the narrative produces two complementary versions of the same story, the tale of how Mr. Chaffanbrass cross-examines witnesses. Starting from this predication as a matrix, we have a scene developing the predicate, a witness being tortured "till he forgets his right hand from his left, till his mind be turned into chaos . . . and then let him give evidence."[6] A scene follows in which Mr. Chaffanbrass is described as torturer and as cat playing with a mouse. Then the two are conflated from the standpoint of the public ("Men congregate to hear him turn a witness inside out. This Mr. Chaffanbrass knows . . . [and] never allows himself to grow dull over his work"). Now a climax occurs: his "turning black into white, winning as an epic solitary hero a fight against three personified allegories, Justice with her sword raised, Truth, and Mercy." Next the anticlimax follows: this champion of bad causes, "proudly conscious he is no little man," is, by contrast, in person "a very dirty little man"— hence, a description that emphasizes the contrast between a mean appearance and a powerful mind. Finally, a corrective: at home, he is "the most . . . amiable old gentleman that ever was pooh-poohed by his grown up daughters" (ibid.). Anticlimax and corrective both have the same motivation: if characters are important or larger than life, verisimilitude will be achieved by making them complex and contradictory. This conforms to a commonsense template: reality is full of contrasts.

What I have described now serves, in turn, as a narrative model for a different mimesis: the novel tells the story of the actual trial, during which Mr. Chaffanbrass will chaff and chafe and be brassy and brazen, according to the premise of his name.

I have dwelt upon this passage from name to function, from function to the predicate that actualizes it, from predicate to its textual transformations, both in theory and then in practice, in order to point to the link between lexical saturation and syntactic derivation. Once truth is given as a type, *in abstracto*, and once this given is consequently marked as fictional, verisimilitude is recovered through textual expansion and repetition of the given. Repetition covers all possibilities from like to like, or from contrary to contrary. The narrative can also be seen as the testing of a hypothesis. The sememe that serves as the starting point or generator functions like a theorem. Its textual transformation is experimental, like a laboratory demonstration in which cultures are replaced with situations and locales.

The examples I have adduced so far are all tinged with humor. This is due, in part, to the corpus from which they have been culled. From the late eighteenth century to the Victorian era in England and to Proust in France (excepting, of course, the Naturalist movement), humor permeates the novel. But there is a reason for the importance of humor that transcends the interplay of historical influence. As a form, as a type of discourse, it neatly distinguishes between the characters' views, concerns, and involvements and, on the other hand, the outsider's viewpoint, the above-the-fray stance, and even the condescension of the narrator.

Among the minor characters in Marcel Proust's vast novel there is a M. Nissim Bernard, whose role in the narrative is determined by his having the triple handicap of being a Jew in an anti-Semitic society, a homosexual in a world of closets, and old, which is the principal determinant of his personal epic because his age prevents him from finding fulfillment in love and forces him to resort to venality and to a willingness to take risks in order to achieve a meager measure of satisfaction.

> Albertine and I were waiting at the Balbec station of the little local railway. We had driven there in the hotel omnibus, because it was raining. Not far away from us was M. Nissim Bernard, who had a black eye. He had recently forsaken the chorister from *Athalie* for the waiter at a much frequented farmhouse in the neighborhood, known as the "Cherry Orchard." This rubicund youth, with his blunt features, appeared for all the world to have a tomato instead of a head. A tomato exactly similar served as head to his twin brother. To the detached observer, the charm of these perfect resemblances between twins is that nature, as if momentarily industrialized, seems to be turning out identical products. Unfortunately M. Nissim Bernard looked at it from another point of view, and this resemblance was only external. Tomato No. 2 showed a frenzied zeal in catering exclusively to the pleasures of ladies; Tomato No. 1 was not averse to complying with the tastes of certain gentlemen. Now on every occasion when, stirred, as though by a reflex, by the memory of pleasant hours spent with Tomato No. 1, M. Bernard presented himself at the Cherry Orchard, being short-sighted (not that one had to be short-sighted to mistake them), the old Jewish gentleman, unwittingly playing Amphitryon, would accost the twin brother with: "Will you meet me somewhere this evening?" He at once received a thorough "hiding." It might even be repeated in the course of a single meal, when he continued with the second brother a conversation he had begun with the first.[7]

The humor is clearly supported by a tradition that goes all the way back to Plautus's *Menaechmi* and that includes the

Amphitryon of Molière, to which the text alludes. These stories all tell of the tribulations of a lover unhappy enough to focus on two look-alike objects of desire, twins or supernatural doubles. The use of tomatoes as a vehicle for a hyperbolic and comical metaphor of confusingly identical twins is no more than the terminal and highest point of a paradigm of such representations. The shift from metaphor to metonymy, however, although it serves as a concession to representation, simply exhausts the topic while dealing a death blow to verisimilitude. Truth, however, triumphs, and the whole episode can be reduced to a matter of style, of form. As content, it is true twice over: it is true that members of persecuted groups tend to make light of their predicament, thus defusing it somewhat. The defusing is thus the real object of the representation, an interpretation of reality rather than reality itself. But as Proust himself liked to say, the business of literary art is not the representation of things but of the impression they make on us or of the way in which we react to them.

It is normal for a good story, for a joke, to build to a punchline, and therefore one further incident may be true again despite its fictionality—at any rate, true to form. The added incident is true, at second remove and twice over—first, as the retelling of a joke that refers to a psychological truth, and, second, despite the parody, as a reflection of a fact of experience. I am referring to the later scene in which M. Nissim Bernard takes his revenge:

> In the end this treatment, by association of ideas, so put him off tomatoes, even of the edible variety, that whenever he heard a newcomer order that vegetable at a neighbouring table in the Grand Hotel, he would murmur to him: "You must excuse me, Monsieur, for addressing you without an introduction. But I heard you order tomatoes. They are bad to-day. I tell you in your own interest; for it makes no difference to me, I never touch them myself." The stranger would thank this philanthropic and dis-

interested neighbor effusively, call back the waiter, and pretend to have changed his mind: "No, on second thought, definitely no tomatoes." Aimé, who had seen it all before, would laugh to himself, and think: "He's an old rascal, that Monsieur Bernard, he's gone and made another of them change his order."[8]

The clausula may be true mimetically, that is, psychologically. Its narrative function is to provide the pseudo-story, the ostensibly fictional *tomato* construct, with a punchline, however, and at the same time to reintegrate it into verisimilitude, since such a scene can be observed not just in confrontations with waiters but on the daily occasions when one covers up the fact that someone else has taken the initiative, knew more, and made a decision that we then maintain to be our own.

The scene is made even more convincing by its being topped or guaranteed by the character of the witness, of the *maître d'*, whose role is to imply a habitual behavior on the part of the protagonist and who is therefore a symbol of that protagonist's reality. The derivation at the very apogee of its production thus reintegrates the episode into the story and further presupposes truth at the point of its maximal fictionality. Aimé belongs to the class of secondary characters who almost act as stagehands, whose reappearances provide background links between principal actors or whose comments indicate some quality in a major actor. That actor's persona would not be fully understood without the minor witness whose role is to notice it.

Humor is especially truth-creating when it verges on mockery. One can admire or praise an ideal or hypothetical character. One can say anything of characters who are present without being fully drawn, who are vague and unverifiable (even in derivations issuing from them), so long as what is said conforms to the logic of mimesis and pragmatic constraints of usage in describing people.

But humor presupposes a truth, since there cannot be a comical way of speaking about an object without first assuming that object's existence. We have to recognize a narrative sequence or a descriptive pattern in its "natural," that is, non-humorous, form, in order to identify the distorting constants or recurrent displacements (for instance, the use of lowbrow metonyms to denote highbrow concepts). We perceive humor as a special case of similarly oriented successive substitutions: we do not have to actualize a neutral way of saying the same things, or simply another way that would seem more normal instead of being preinterpreted, as it were, or laudatory instead of being irreverent. We are simply aware after the fact of whatever wording might have been more expected. Humor, then, rests on the existence of another way of saying or of being that exists prior to the application of its distorting system or lexical grid to that representation. This assumed preexistence (perhaps an actual one in the genesis of the text, but even that would entail a logical inference in the reader's interpretation of that text) now turns into a presupposition of objective reality. Such a reality is anterior and exterior to the subject's perception of it, and to our reading of that perception, to our reading of that presupposed object through the narrator's subjectivizing lens.

Here is an example from Dickens's *Little Dorrit*. The target of the narrator's mirth is the wife of the great financier, Mr. Merdle, "a man of prodigious enterprise; a Midas without the ears, who turned all he touched to gold . . . He was in everything good, from banking to building.[9] Our first sight of Mrs. Merdle is this:

> The lady was not young and fresh from the hand of Nature, but was young and fresh from the hand of her maid. She had large unfeeling handsome eyes, and dark unfeeling handsome hair, and a broad unfeeling handsome bosom.
>
> (Ibid., chap. 20, 221)

She is sitting "in a nest of crimson and gold cushions on an ottoman near the parrot" (ibid., 222). From this first glimpse through approximately six hundred thirty pages, encounters with Mrs. Merdle will occasionally draw a parallel between her and the parrot in its gilded cage and will constantly replace the whole of her rich person with an especially conspicuous and significant synecdoche, her décolleté. Conspicuousness and significance are inseparable here, since her deep cleavage stands for her at two levels: diegetically, it is a metonym of the lady as a sex object and, narratively, it is motivated as one of the showcases of Mr. Merdle's wealth:

> This great and fortunate man had provided that extensive bosom, which required so much room to be unfeeling enough in, with a nest of crimson and gold some fifteen years before. It was not a bosom to repose upon, but it was a capital bosom to hang jewels upon. Mr. Merdle wanted something to hang jewels upon, and he bought it for the purpose . . . Like all his other speculations, it was sound and successful . . . The bosom moving in Society with the jewels displayed upon it attracted general admiration.
>
> (Ibid., chap. 21, 230)

The narrative function of this showcase is reactivated throughout the novel, humor here being the stylistic means of social satire, a prop in the comedy of manners. The metonymic function, however, is the prime generator for the series, and I think it is the key both to fictionality and to truth as two facets of the same device. In the introductory quotation ("She had large unfeeling handsome eyes and dark unfeeling handsome hair, and a broad unfeeling handsome bosom"), the repetition of *handsome* is normal. Not so that of *unfeeling:* Its repetition must therefore be laden with significance. To be sure, the adjective is appropriate to *eyes*, since with that word, the proairesis keeps options open between coldness and sensitivity. Unfeeling, however, is inappropriate to or even nonsensical with *hair*, and it verges on the oxymoric with *bosom*, to the point of ungrammaticality. For the essential semes of that sememe make it the quintessential sign for warmth and love: *bosom* stands for woman as a mother and/or as a lover; *bosom* is the equivalent of "feeling" in *body* code.

Hence the power of the reversal transforming *bosom* into a paradoxical symbol of coldness, hence the negative valorization that it will take the whole series of appearances of Mrs. Merdle as jewelry stand to exhaust. Hence, to begin with, a crazy story out of nowhere, the invention of a whole past life for Mrs. Merdle, whose function is to motivate the coldness necessary for her character to conform to the novel's telos. A male Merdle, insensitive exploiter of people, demands a female counterpart. Consequently, the story provides him with a wife not actively noxious, because she is there only to complete his image as an established paragon of social life, as a married man; but a cold man must have a frigid woman—a heartless speculator, a wife with a heart of ice. The culmination of this paradigm is also the narrative motivation, the most farfetched motivation imaginable for that bosom's unbosomy coldness:

> Mrs. Merdle's first husband had been a colonel, under whose auspices the bosom had entered into competition with the snows of North America, and had come off at little disadvantage in point of whiteness, and at none in point of coldness.
>
> (Ibid.)

It is true that the novel needs to create a stepson for Mrs. Merdle, a vapid youngster who has to be saved from "being monomaniacal in offering marriage to all manner of undesirable young ladies" (ibid., 231). But this secondary telos could easily have been fulfilled without inventing a Canadian or North American first career for Mrs. Merdle. The only reason for this diegetic detour is that North American snows are exemplary in the nineteenth-century British sociolect. Transposed into a *before/after* cause and effect consecution, the snows admirably motivate Mrs. Merdle's coldness via a simile bridging the gap between the two basic, and therefore easily related, literary whitenesses of winter and feminine skin.

The significance of the paradigm of variations on Mrs. Merdle's bosom is the inversion of a cliché for warmth and love, and that is the truth of the motif, the truth of so many oxymorons of literature: the cankerworm in the rose, the soft heart of the criminal, the golden heart of the prostitute, cruelty in love, kindness in a brute, etc. As for the humor, Dickens's method throughout the novel is to alternate melodrama and comedy in pursuing the same satirical goals. Merdle is savaged, Mrs. Merdle is mocked, and both portrayals are equally destructive. A single isolated depiction of Mrs. Merdle as bosom would have been a serious indictment. The repeated reduction of the whole person to a part of her body is fun. As is usual with repetition, it has a momentum of its own, not so much in terms of dynamics as in terms of analogy. On the model of a person reduced to a cleavage and of the cleavage reduced to the jewels bedecking it, we will find a guest at a dinner party whispering sweet nothings not into Mrs. Merdle's ear, but "at Mrs. Merdle's nearest ear-ring" (ibid., bk. 2, chap. 25, 663). Again, on the model of another reduction, there is the comparison between Mrs. Merdle in her nest of cushions and the parrot next to her. A new visitor to that lady's boudoir will find the "parrot on a neighbouring stem watching her with his head on one side, as if he took her for another splendid parrot of a larger species." (ibid., bk. 1, chap. 33, 470). The generative power of the paradigm is here further demonstrated by this mirror image: as the narrative runs out of possible situations to develop by analogy, it creates one more version by inverting the terms of the initial predication linking the two actors (it is now the woman who parrots the parrot).

The consequence of repetition, either of structurally identical elements in the guise of variation or of the same figure (for instance, metonymic reification that equates woman with jeweler's window) in different situations, of a continuity in various contexts not unlike a sustained metaphor strewn through the whole novel—in short, the uniformly humorous slant maintained from one moment in a narrative sequence to the next—this is the index of fictionality. Verisimilitude requires an adjustment to each successive context, a new lighting of the stage, a descriptive response to the demands of evolving motivation and, specifically, varying viewpoints with changing actors and changing interplay between them. The continuity that generates humor cannot therefore be anything other than the voice of an outsider, that is to say, the narrator's viewpoint, the distancing of the author from his fiction.

Humor as an index of fictionality is not necessarily repetitive, even though this type is the most important in the narrative, because narrative is successive, and the unfolding of a repetitive sequence creates a contrast so fundamental between these two intertwined linear developments that if the function of the first sequence is to emphasize verisimilitude, the second is bound to do the opposite.

One more type of humor can be defined as authorial intrusion or as a sign of the narrator distancing himself from the narration. It consists in a diegetic derivation that treats an ostensibly hypothetical or figurative statement of the *as if* kind as if it were real.

In *Illusions Perdues*, immediately following the portrait of Séchard the drunkard, Balzac depicts visitors going through the man's printing shop. The point of the story is mimetic:

people in provincial towns are supposed to be more curious about trades and techniques than denizens of the big city. The whole passage is full of repeated evidence of how easily surprised and excited the good bourgeois are by the printing presses and other contraptions:

> Here, too, the forms, or, in ordinary language, the masses of set-up type, were washed. Inky streams issuing thence blended with the ooze from the kitchen sink, and found their way into the gutter in the street outside; till peasants coming into the town on market day believed that the devil was having a wash inside the establishment.[10]

This, of course, is bound to be a joke. Not even the most primitive peasants could have believed this. The detail is meant to cap a sequence about visitors marveling at this or that machine and being made fun of by the workmen who are amused by their simplemindedness and lack of technical knowledge. Indeed, the detail hyperbolizes in one last variant a constant of the narrative (the outsiders getting an education). Humor here imposes the narrator upon the workman, as it were, as if his joke were the extreme point reachable by the repetitive story—a last variant added metalinguistically, in the margin, concluding by a shift into the narrator's voice, and therefore by fiction, instead of concluding with a blank margin.

And yet, once more, as verisimilitude stops at the penultimate variant of the paradigm, truth takes over through an analogy. Peasants are supposed to be less sophisticated than townspeople, and it may be said that, on the scale of gullibility, to believe in the devil is to the peasants what to wonder at techniques is to the bourgeois. The conventional portrait of a primitive, now patently anachronistic and implausible, functions as a representation *in abstracto* of puzzlement or insecurity in the presence of novelty.

Here, however, the narrator's intrusion is still connected with the textual sequence through a shared structure. The fictionalizing derivation can be absolutely devoid of reference, and thus demonstrably unacceptable while still being verifiable. In the portrait of the drunkard already cited, Balzac seems to follow a highly predictable pattern in recounting the progress of Séchard's addiction:

> His wife, during her lifetime, managed to control within reasonable bounds his passion for the juice of the grape, and taste so natural to the bear that M. de Chateaubriand remarked it among the ursine tribes of the New World. But the philosophers inform us that old age is apt to revert to the habits of youth, and Séchard senior is a case in point—the older he grew, the better he loved to drink.[11]

Again, there is no way we can take this seriously. The allusion to Chateaubriand's narrative of his travels in America makes use of a quotation that has provoked mirth ever since the publication of that illustrious volume. Chateaubriand claimed to have seen, in the depth of the American forest, bears tipsy because they had eaten too many grapes. This was too farfetched for French readers, and perhaps even inaccurate. In any case, the proof has the value of an empty or symbolic gesture of reference to sources, that is to say, none at all. But then the link between *a taste so natural* and Chateaubriand's fanciful plantigrades is *bear,* which would be nonsensical if we had not learned a few lines before that in printers' slang the name for Séchard's speciality (worker in charge of inking the press) was *bear.* Furthermore, a joking pseudo-learned word for *drunkenness* in colloquial French is *soûlographie,* a compound of *saoul,* "drunk," and the suffix *-graphy* as in *typography.* Balzac has just played on this parallelism: "Séchard was better at *tipple-ography,* if I may say, than at *typography.*" All this is quite definitely a metalanguage belonging to the author himself, but it is also a symbolic tautology, valid only through the positing of a joke that makes it possible to equate an imaginary animal (Chateaubriand's furry drunk) and a metaphorical bear (Balzac's human drunk). We are thus faced with an impregnable symbolic logic: if Séchard is as much of a bear as Chateaubriand's bears, then he is as typically addicted to drink as they.

More often than not, humor extends to the whole of a novel. In contrast, the third and last category of fictional indices never goes beyond the limits of a subtext. In fact, it generates subtexts and is therefore the most widespread type of fictional deixis. Chief among signs of fictionality are those stylistic traits, especially figures and tropes, that are inconsistent with the narrative situation or with a character's speech or station in life. I am not speaking of features that are the imprint of the writer's personality or the fingerprint from which readers learn to recognize a novel as representative of its author. Nor am I speaking of formal constants that transcribe into the narrative the stylistic profile of the narrator's persona. Nor do I have in mind the figurative means and the tropology used in the text (attributable or not to a narrator's persona or simply construed in the third person) to enliven the story or to animate characters. The latter devices are often inconsistent with an objective telling or with the viewpoint that characters involved in the action might have about ongoing events. They are often incompatible with what characters know of themselves, with what their psychological or social portrait would suggest, or with what thoughts are attributed to them.

I would like to make a distinction between incompatibilities signaled and underscored by a tropological modifier and incompatibilities originating with a shift from the narrator's voice to a character's voice that is not immediately perceived, but with which readers have, sooner or later, to come to terms. The signal in this second category is a zero-signal, a perfect diegetic/stylistic blend and thus an invisible seam in the narrative fabric. It is a smooth transition from narrator to character or the other way around, so smooth, so easy that it is only because the resulting derivation is illogical that we take notice of it, and we do so only after the fact.

My example of a trope-induced incompatibility is one of Marcel Proust's best-defined subtexts: its diegesis is triggered by a given that is literal and therefore rooted in verisimilitude. The generation of the subtext from that matrix, however, is regulated by a metaphorical reinterpretation of the given.

This subtext involves the cameo appearance of two members of the old French nobility, two ladies with walking sticks. They are so inseparable from these sticks that they are ultimately identified with these metonyms of themselves and represent a human species or at least subspecies known as *dames à cannes.* This metonymy, and its narrative function in the novel, is deduced from metaphorical descriptions that develop this one metonymic word into a whole text.

When the narrator first meets these ladies, he discovers that, far from suggesting a crippled physique, these sticks indicate a strong constitution and purposeful mind. He muses about the number of similar persons in the aristocratic neighborhood of the *faubourg St.-Germain,* wondering whether this statistical quirk is due to the fact that noble-women are likely to break their legs riding to hounds or whether the dampness of their ancestral châteaux has stiffened their joints. The two ladies are trying to convince the Duc de Guermantes not to go to a costume ball because of the imminent death of a cousin. Their devotion to upholding family self-respect coincides with the metamorphosis of their walking sticks into climbing sticks:

The duke was rather curt with them. And so, although they had come down from the heights of the Hotel de Bréquigny . . . to announce to the Duchess the alarming character, incompatible for his relatives with attendance at social affairs, of their cousin's illness, they did not stay long: each armed with her climbing stick, Walpurge and Dorothée retraced the craggy path to their mountain top [*elles reprirent la route escarpée de leur faîte*].[12]

The count's townhouse is only a few blocks away from the duke's in the same neighborhood of splendid residences and private gardens. The modest hills of the Left Bank in Paris do not reach for the sky, nor do they offer crags and cliffs. The dizzying heights suggested by the joke about alpenstocks arise from a descriptive detail, or rather from a metaphor depicted in painterly discourse. A few pages earlier the narrator had been looking at the skyline from his window. From that vantage point, the perspective makes the two ladies' mansion appear farther and higher than it actually is:

> Between me and this house . . . [there were] nothing but blocks of buildings . . . which prolonged the distance with their oblique planes. The red tiled turret of the coachhouse . . . reminded one of those picturesque old buildings in Switzerland which spring up in isolation at the foot of a mountain. All these vague and divergent points . . . made . . . the house, actually quite near, but misleadingly distant as in an Alpine landscape, appear as though it were separated from us . . . by a series of foothills.[13]

Thus the ladies' sticks and their ascent are born of a metaphorical rationalization of the actual sticks. They are only a trope. And now, in a second step, the narrative and its diegetic universe are generated by a literal reinterpretation of that trope: the movement is from literality to figurative discourse to literality again.

Whatever verisimilitude remains is now challenged by a

third rationalization that makes it depend on yet another figure, one that presupposes an interpretation, namely, an ekphrasis, the verbal representation of visual art. The metaphorical tableau of a mountain landscape is motivated by this imaginary ekphrasis:

> in following from one floor to the next the footmen whom it was impossible to see clearly but who were visibly shaking carpets, one felt the same pleasure as when one sees in a landscape by Turner or Elstir a traveller in a stagecoach, or a guide, at different degrees of altitude on the slopes of a mountain pass.[14]

Now that the pseudo-landscape is proven true by these references, replacing an actual referentiality that has become entirely pointless, we come to the realization of the narrative telos, the upright morality that our sturdy climbers embody. The duke is rushing home from a formal dinner in order to put on his costume for the masked ball he has prepared for with such obstinate levity:

> He ran into the ladies with the walking-sticks outside his door which they were grimly guarding. They had not been afraid to descend in the dead of night from their mountain top to prevent a scandal. "Basin, we felt we must warn you that you must not be seen at that ball. Poor Amanien has just died, an hour ago." The Duke was momentarily dismayed. He saw the famous ball ruined for him now that these accursed mountaineers had informed him of M. d'Osmond's death. But he quickly recovered himself and flung at his cousins a retort which reflected, together with his determination not to forgo a pleasure, his inability to master the niceties of the French language: "He is dead! No, no, they exaggerate, they exaggerate!"[15]

The words *these accursed mountaineers* are clearly attributed to the duke. They are not said aloud, but represent his train of thought, the barely repressed voice of his inner rage. Just as clearly, this attribution has to be humorous, since the

Duc de Guermantes is not privy to the narrator's mind and it is only on the horizon of that mind that the mountains have risen. The syntax belongs to one character, the lexicon to another, the narrator. Only one viewpoint can reconcile the two, that of the author.

The author, therefore, or his persona, becomes one more index of truth, since he represents the metalinguistic locus in which the initial trope (the ladies as mountaineers) takes shape (the metalanguage of this rationalization), thereby presupposing the factuality of female cane wielders in aristocratic circles. Furthermore, the truth thus presupposed can convincingly generate a text only because of the text's sociolectic authority: a cliché image of older women in families, interestingly indomitable despite the dual frailty of age and of gender and their traditional role as upholders of proprieties, the Vestals of modern times.

In summary, fictional indices have both a diegetic and a logical function. As descriptive components, they depart from the narrative's consecution enough to expose its artifice. As tropes that are unacceptable within narrative conventions, they presuppose the real, the given that tropes need as a foil.

Three

Symbolic Systems in Narrative

All truth-creating devices discussed so far are directly related to verisimilitude proper, whether in its pure form or combined with indices of fictionality. There is, however, another category of truth devices based on symbolism, or rather on sign systems that are embedded in the fictional text, yet clearly differentiated from it. Such sign systems provide a metalinguistic commentary that points to the truth of the context surrounding them. These systems possess a self-contained verisimilitude that follows the rules I have discussed in the first two chapters. But each of them remains a separate unit of significance and, as such, an outside commentary on the truth of fiction, symbolizing it in a different discourse. The relationship of these systems to the narrative is not unlike that of poetic to cognitive discourse.

Save for occasional coincidences, the symbolic systems

of narrative that I propose to examine have nothing to do with what some critics still call the symbolism of a novel as a whole, or of a particular episode, or of a character. I take it that this practice is meant loosely to refer to the kind of habitual significance that we attach to certain signs apart from their own meaning or use, and sometimes even at odds with that meaning.

Symbolic systems are more specific. They must be understood as networks of signs, each organized by an ad hoc grammar that does not supersede the grammar of the context surrounding the system but that may suspend or modify some of its rules.

Two such systems have the function of injecting a qualitatively different truth, a poetic truth, into a world of truth by verisimilitude: the sustained metaphor and the subtext. They are both prolonged sequences, and often dispersed, since their components may be separated by contextual gaps, strewn along the progression of the linear narrative. Both, therefore, focus the readers' attention by repeating forms and contents. Their own individual grammar thus follows the general rule of tautological derivation, but their respective derivations are woven in and out of the main narrative derivations without mixing with them, just as an undercurrent flows visibly distinct from the surrounding river. Both offer a second or metalinguistic reading of what the text surrounding them is about, thus creating a frame of referentiality. It is, indeed, only a frame or a model rather than a substance of referentiality, like a gesture that points to something we have to assume is anterior and exterior to the referring text and that, therefore, constitutes an authority for whatever that text narrates.

Sustained metaphors can be found in texts other than narrative, but subtexts are indigenous to narrative. I have proposed to define them as those narrative units of significance that account for readers' ability to find their way unerringly

FICTIONAL TRUTH

in fiction.[1] The many leads fiction offers to interpretation and the great length of most works of fiction would make them unmanageable, and the unity one expects in a work of art would remain unperceived without texts within the text embedded in the fabric of the whole novel. Subtexts function like syntagms embedded in the fabric of a larger syntagm, playing in it the role of lexemes, as if they themselves were words, only more complex, since they actually are periphrastic substitutes for words. Immersed in the overall fictional sequence, they are derived from the same matrix as the whole narrative or from a matrix structurally connected models of reading, as hermeneutic guideposts, not unlike themes or motifs, except that a theme or motif has a matrix themes or motifs, except that a theme or motif has a matrix of its own that is born elsewhere and exists before that of the larger text. Themes and motifs therefore function, in effect, as if they were quotations. The subtext could stand alone and be remembered as an episode may be remembered, except that an episode is a link in a chain of events, while a subtext is no such thing, since it can be omitted without unraveling the fabric or obscuring the logic of the narrative. Finally, subtexts are not solid entities; they are, as I have said, dispersed along the narrative, either because their development is interrupted and the thread picked up later, or because a subtext reappears in successive variants like a paradigm of synonymic statements. A subtext's symbolic system has two characteristic features: being idiosyncratic, it becomes increasingly difficult to understand unless one connects it with the previous occurrences; and because of this, it works like a memory built into the narrative.

A subtext is always structured on a polar opposition between a relatively unimportant topic and a wide-ranging hermeneutic function. Nothing could suit my demonstration better than the following example from E. M. Forster's *A*

Passage to India. The nub of the subtext, which seems like a figurative justification of the prefix *sub* in *subtext*, is, symbolically enough, the most minute part of a man's clothing, not even a button; it is a stud. The significance encompasses the whole British empire, colonial India, the Raj, and its multivolume trail of novels. The story is about the hopeless impossibility of bridging the gap between the East and the West, at least, our West as it is modeled on what is left of the white man's burden principle, or on what kept this principle alive enough in 1924 to make it a valid object of mimesis and a challenging target of satire. Forster built his novel on a negative or pessimistic reading of the positive program of exciting exoticism evoked by Whitman in the poem from which the novel gets its title. The reading is negative, but it is also funny, sympathetic, light-hearted, and even poetic.

A Mohammedan doctor is devoured by the anxious desire to be accepted as an equal on the same terms as those that obtain among the British in their own world. On the occasion of his first meeting with an open-minded British teacher, one who is almost free of bias, Dr. Aziz demonstrates how far he is from the race that has conquered his land. He does nothing wrong; he is just so un-British. His enthusiasm for his new friend, a man whom he has never before seen, but has heard about, is fulsome and his eagerness pathetic, or at any rate it is just that, eagerness. One should not be eager. Aziz is basking in the pleasure of being Mr. Fielding's guest. The moment is ripe for the incident that summarizes everything and generates what I will call the *collar stud* subtext. Fielding is still in his dressing room, talking to Aziz through the ground glass:

> "Blast!"
> "Anything wrong?"
> "I've stamped on my last collar stud."

"Take mine, take mine."

"Have you a spare one?"

"Yes, yes, one minute."

"Not if you're wearing it yourself."

"No, no, one in my pocket." Stepping aside, so that his outline might vanish, he wrenched off his collar, and pulled out of his shirt the back stud, a gold stud, which was part of a set that his brother-in-law had brought him from Europe. "Here it is," he cried.

"Come in with it if you don't mind the unconventionality."

"One minute again." Replacing his collar, he prayed that it would not spring up at the back during tea. Fielding's bearer, who was helping him to dress, opened the door for him.

"Many thanks." They shook hands smiling. He began to look round, as he would have with any old friend. Fielding was not surprised at the rapidity of their intimacy. With so emotional a people it was apt to come at once or never.[2]

Twenty pages later, the local British administrator, the epitome of the self-confident colonial, laughs at the very idea that Dr. Aziz could actually invite British women to a tour in the country. Revealingly, his irony takes the form of a reference to the collar stud:

"Have I said anything funny?"

"I was only thinking how the worthy doctor's collar climbed up his neck."

". . . Aziz was exquisitely dressed, from tie-pin to spats, but he had forgotten his back collar-stud, and there you have the Indian all over: inattention to detail; the fundamental slackness that reveals the race."

(Ibid., chap. 8, 81–82)

Ten pages later, a conversation takes place after a hard day's work preventing a religious riot:

Ronny [the British city magistrate] had not disliked his day, for it proved that the British were necessary to India; there would certainly have been bloodshed without them. His voice grew complacent again; . . . "Incredible, aren't they, even the best of them? They're all—they all forget their back collar studs sooner or later."

(Ibid., 96)

A minor symbol, to be sure, but one that entirely sums up everything that separates two worlds and that works despite its puny size as the touchstone to test the minds, or rather the souls, of three or four characters. A minor incident, but one that affords the text a chance to develop fully: (1) psychological analysis; (2) the semiotics of racial behavior; (3) a comedy of manners; (4) a touching scene, but a silly one as well; (5) the irony of fate. The collar does climb up the neck, and Aziz's sweet, if perhaps embarrassing, gesture hilariously becomes the cause of misunderstanding, a looming racial barrier (the natives cannot remember what collar studs are for). The count of consequences continues: (6) a mimesis of class blindness; and (7) the pathos of bad will following that of good will. The subtext therefore contains in a nutshell all the ingredients that make the novel work. Everything that it will take the whole second part of the novel (180 pages) to develop, all the way to the melodramatic climax (an accusation of interracial rape), every episode and every motivation finds itself foretold, mirrored in the little gold knob.

What constitutes a subtext? What rule or rules can account for its hermeneutic function, for that function's relevance to a whole novel and to the fictionality of that novel? First a subtext centers on a minor object or event, or on an unimportant character, hardly more than a stagehand, and if it does concern the protagonist's personality or actions, it still focuses on what would in the real world be a negligible aspect. The subtext thus revolves around a mimesis that plays in the narrative a role akin to that of the realistic detail in the descriptive. In both cases, there is, at first glance, the insignificance, an insignificance that we deduce from the context and also from the rules of behavior in our lives and from the value or non-value such details receive from the sociolect's ideological framework, from their practical uselessness and resulting near-invisibility in that framework. In both cases, this insignificance leaves them free to assume an enormous ad hoc, context-dictated significance. In the descriptive, the detail represents truth itself, uninterpreted existence, almost an essence of being, simply because no narrative motivation for it is imaginable, no hint that it could serve the purpose of encoding an intention, of manipulating the reader in view of the novel's telos. In the narrative, the subtext connects its own topic or its minidrama metonymically, metaphorically, or symbolically with one of the novel's sequences of events or even with the main sequence, and with the telos of each.

This insignificance/significance dialectic clearly separates the concept of subtext from the accepted categories of theme and motif. A theme is immediately and conspicuously important. It articulates at the diegetic level a sequence of events also articulated at the narrative level by the basic overall structure of the novel. Consequently, every variation on the theme refers to or makes direct use of the principal supply of representations, literal or figurative, required by the verisimilitude of the story and of its characters. A motif, on the other hand, is unimportant except inasmuch as it is repeated, and it remains unimportant: the effect of its repetition is stylistic, and sometimes it suggests an esthetic or moral coloration, an atmosphere, a truth of mood.

The novel's female protagonist, for instance, the young British woman, panics in the dark during a tour of religious caves up in the primeval hills above the British station. She imagines that she has been molested, and perhaps she has. A primary cause for her mental confusion is the echo inside the caves. A long initial description of the outer sound becomes a pathological inner obsession:

> Even the striking of a match starts a little worm coiling . . . And if several people talk at once, . . . echoes generate echoes, and the cave is stuffed with a snake composed of small snakes, which writhe independently.
>
> (Ibid., chap. 7, 72)

The narrative returns again and again to this event, until the mind of the victim echoes the echo, with her suffering an unbearable ringing in the ears that will stop only when she publicly admits in court that she has accused her alleged aggressor wrongly. This is no subtext, but an iterative variation on an experience central to the thoughts and motives of a central character.

My second point towards a definition of the subtext as the quintessential, defining unit of narrative fictionality is that it is a form rather than a content. No matter how often it reappears, the same form makes it recognizable, whether its return is complete or fragmentary. That again distinguishes the subtext from a theme. Although a theme is essentially a story, or a fragment of a story, that develops an aspect of the main plot, its recurrences admit of many shapes. In *A Passage to India*, the tropical heat is, naturally enough, a recurring theme: it is consistently represented through a succession of violent efforts to find the right image for a power so alien to the Western reader's experience that no ordinary or familiar mimesis of our dog days would be equal to it. This goes on as if the very multiformity of the diegesis had for its object less the summer in the subcontinent than the hopelessness of ever adequately representing it.

In a way, the subtext resembles a sustained metaphor,

with the difference, however, that that kind of metaphor remains subordinated to whatever narrative sequence has resorted to it for its diegetic implementation. Our Mohammedan hero, Dr. Aziz, is given to moments of happy delusion, when, for instance, he glories in playing host to the British women and initiating them into the splendors of the Indian past—hence, an image for the purpose of separating exaltation from fact. One of the ladies

> supposed him to be emancipated as well as reliable, and placed him on a pinnacle which he could not retain. He was high enough for the moment, to be sure, but not on any pinnacle. Wings bore him up, and flagging would deposit him.
>
> (Ibid., chap. 7, 72)

From that passage on, the image of wings is, as it were, borrowed by the narrator from the female character's supposedly private thoughts. Whenever Aziz gets carried away by his enthusiasm, uplifting thoughts are translated into wings lifting him up. So great is the generative power of this given that the image is finally internalized by Aziz's psyche, and he dreams of himself as a true descendant of the Arab conquerors of India. This shift from character to narrator to yet another character is one of the indices of fictionality discussed in the second chapter. But never do the wings acquire a life of their own and become a center for a narrative unit.

The sustained metaphor, however, has another similarity with the subtext besides that of being sustained. As they recur in the narrative, each new version becomes more idiosyncratic in its wording than the previous one, or more elliptical. Each new version of the sustained metaphor, as well as of the subtext, would therefore appear incoherent to a reader unaware of its previous instances. This seems to me to be the key to the subtext's efficacy, to its capacity to have a hermeneutic function and to its capacity to transform insignificance or even nonsense on one level into significance on another.

The first consequence of this gradual increase in difficulty is that the reader has to reread or remember in order to retrieve the sense presupposed by the nonsense. Those critics who make the mistake of judging any passage of a novel independently of the sequence of which it is only a link perversely ignore the sequential, successive nature of narrative. They also ignore the substitutability principle that governs not just the use of tropes but any equivalence a literary text may posit between a first wording and subsequent variants. Sainte-Beuve was egregiously guilty of this double blindness when he chose to censure Balzac for having written in his novel *Le Curé de Tours* the following metaphorical tale about evil gossip in a provincial town[3]:

> such was the substance of the words which the capillary pipes of the great feminine conclave were throwing forth and that were eagerly repeated by the whole town.[4]

My translation cannot do justice to the non sequitur of the image, exacerbated as it is by the periphrasis *tuyaux capillaires*, "capillary pipes," instead of the correct "capillary vessels." The image verges on the conundrum, but as Marcel Proust pointed out when he castigated Sainte-Beuve for reading only the end of a sequence, everything here depends on a perfectly clear and compellingly logical sustained metaphor ten pages earlier:

> These people [inveterate gossips, mostly embittered housewives and frustrated spinsters] all living downtown so as to represent the capillary vessels [here Balzac still uses the acceptable botanical wording] sucked up, with the thirst of leaves for dew, the news and secrets about every household, pumped them and transmitted them machine-like to Father Troubert [a master schemer], the way leaves pass on to the stem the moisture they absorb.[5]

The image may be cumbersome but, as Proust has noted, it is admirably true, clear, and unified. What gives it its unity, of course, is that the figurative is remodeled on the reality it illustrates—or rather, the metaphor closely hugs every clause of the sociolectic stereotypes about circulating gossip or a network of calumny. This is step one of the transformation; step two: any circulation network can easily translate into a vegetable or anatomical vessel network.

For the sake of clarity, I shall briefly formalize the various points I have made about the function of the two symbolic systems. Each one focuses attention on itself as form before it starts operating as content. Form and content have two distinct functions. (1) Form, being obviously contrived, betrays the hand of its maker and signals fictionality; (2) content symbolizes. It may symbolize the telos of the whole story, or an aspect of the plot, or a facet of a character's mind. This symbolic function plays the part of fictional truth (rather than referring to that truth) by appearing exemplary and by presupposing.

Let us now turn to the two mechanisms that link together symbol formation and narrative generation: one is the mnemonic function of the subtext (or to a lesser degree, the mnemonic function of the sustained metaphor—I say to a lesser degree only because a metaphor, however sustained it may be, will never cover as much narrative ground as a subtext). The mnemonic function is the subtext's ability to mobilize or reawaken points of the narrative that had passed unnoticed and now appear at second glance to have been proleptic. The second mechanism that makes symbolism a factor in generating the narrative is the paradigmatic nature of subtext recurrences: each of them signifies in terms of the previous one and all are recognizable as variants of one another. They therefore convey the same symbolism throughout. Each variant, by the very fact that it is variable, adjusts at the diegetic level to any situation, event, or character it may fit. As a result, character, event, or situation is permeated with the invariable symbolism, repeating its lesson or message under the successive disguises of the story's progress.

Hence, there is unity of significance as well as esthetic unity. Moreover, since paradigm and narrative have the common factor of successivity, and since the paradigm has the peculiarity of being repetitive and cumulative, the narrative patterned on the paradigm is accelerated, the effect of subsequent paradigmatic variants is heightened, and the whole series is brought to a climax both formal (humor, for instance) and semiotic (the symbolic content).

All of these phenomena are especially easy to observe in the works of a writer whose argument and narrative constructs are made conspicuous almost as a geometric scheme against a multifarious diegetic background—I have in mind Anthony Trollope, and the example I am proposing is from *He Knew He Was Right*. The central plot spins out the tragic tale of a marriage destroyed by a sincere, honest, but prideful wife whose unbending spirit drives her husband literally to madness. The subplot contrasts this with the happily ending story of a wedding won by the meek Dorothy, whose modesty conquers the hearts of both her lover and her wealthy and cantankerous spinster aunt, old Miss Stanbury. The subplot also brings comic relief to the high drama of the plot. Comedy stems from a subplot within the subplot the diegetic function of which is to bring to the fore Dorothy's simplicity by contrasting it with the cunning affectations of two sisters past their prime. Having learned the hard way "that of all worldly goods a husband is the best,"[6] they vie with each other in trying to catch Mr. Gibson, a minor canon of the cathedral. This is where the derivation from a metonymy transforms the stagy farce—the clergyman's shuttlecock to the Misses Frenches' battledores—into high comedy with psychological truth. The purely mechanical accidents of a circular chase give way to the pathos of emotions and to psychological analysis when these accidents are treated as symbols.

Dorothy's refreshing ingenuousness is symbolized by her "soft hair which [her aunt] loved so well,—because it was a grace given by God and not bought out of a shop" (ibid., chap. 73, 684). Her opposite's crafty snares have a chignon for their emblem, a postiche purchased by Arabella French in an attempt to repair the injuries of Time.

A *chignon* subtext develops this contrast *ad absurdum*. It pushes humor to the verge of low comedy. It brings the picturesque and realism in characterization to the brink of parody via intertexts whose patent, self-centered literariness seems at variance with the relative transparency of a Victorian novel's matter-of-factness. The symbol on which the subtext is centered, the hairpiece, is not just a substitute for and comical reification of the woman who wears it, but, more improbably and thus more comically, it stands in for her as an object of desire. It is as if the unlikely symbolism of a *chignon* had the role of laying bare the repressed sexual realities that the sociolectic discourse of holy matrimony is supposed to sublimate. Despite this challenge to what the context can bear and a disproportion between the thing and its connotations that is worthy of the "Rape of the Lock," the subtext is linked to a narrative and mimetic verisimilitude that is easily woven into the fabric of the tale. It does not threaten the narrative's unity despite its departure from the diegetic norm. Indeed, the symbol appears true, however ludicrous the choice of it may be, because what a chignon tells us about a woman is motivated four hundred pages earlier by old Miss Stanbury's principles of Christian living. Her religion finds such secular adornments iniquitous:

She hated those vile patches,—dirty flat daubs of millinery as she called them; but they had become too general for her to refuse admittance for such a thing within her doors. But a chignon,—a bandbox behind the noddle,—she would not endure.

(Ibid., chap. 8, 74)

As for the adverse effect of the chignon on the prospective mate whom Arabella French hopes to net, it is but a commonplace of drama and of poetic justice that the most clever designs may be counterproductive.

These mitigations of the subtext's more improbable developments remain secondary, however. Its essential or primary truth stems from humor itself, for humor in its very excess appears to be the faithful representation of panic anxiety. The situation is comical for the outsider and the reader, but cruelly true for the characters. So it is for the woman fishing for a husband. Indeed, Trollope seems to renounce all stylistic restraints, taking the fish and bait image to the letter. He dares to speak of Arabella "landing the scaly darling out of the fresh and free waters of his bachelor stream, and sousing him into the pool of domestic life" (ibid., chap. 47, 443). The crazily sustained metaphor is made worse by the allusion to the amorous queen's soliloquy in *Antony and Cleopatra* (act 2, scene 5) where Shakespeare has his heroine mix graphic literality and metaphorical aptness:

I will betray   11
Tawny-finn'd fishes, my bended hook shall pierce
Their slimy jaws; and as I draw them up,
I'll think them every one an Antony
And say "Ah, ha! y'are caught."   15

The superimposition and the unlikely image may be grotesque, but as the mimesis of a mental state, this grotesqueness betrays the quickening pace of maddened obsession.

A similar development in poor Gibson's mind parallels

hers with *his* obsession. He magnifies the chignon's "shapeless excrescence" into a "distorted monster," growing "bigger and bigger, more shapeless, monstrous, absurd, and abominable, as he looked at it" (ibid., 443). The style is bloated, but it is only consistent with the rise of paranoia and the sexual nature of the threat that triggers it. As the victim has to face the thought of connubial intimacies, the chignon nightmarishly replaces and embodies the bride. We come as close to lifting the veil on nuptial mysteries as Victorian prudishness would allow:

> And as he regarded it in a *nearer and dearer light,*—as a chignon that might possibly *become his own,* as a burden which in one sense he might himself be called upon to bear, as a domestic utensil of which he himself might be called upon to inspect, and, perhaps, to aid the shifting on and shifting off, he did begin to think that that side of the Scylla gulf ought to be avoided if possible.
>
> (Ibid., chap. 47, 440)

Then, for the second time in the same page, Trollope's sense of stylistic balance seems to desert him, as literary parody compounds humor. But this last twist is merely an example of a derivative paradigm symbolically reaching the limits of language. English no longer suffices, Vergil is called into play, and the chignon looms above Gibson like the Cyclops over Ulysses:

> He thought that he never in his life had seen anything so unshapely as that huge wen at the back of her head. "Monstrum horrendum, informe, ingens!" He could not help quoting the words to himself.
>
> (Ibid., 441)

By now the reader is carried along irresistibly and finds it natural for the metonymy to have become almost a vision, a visitation from the foul fiend: "Poor young woman,— perishing beneath an incubus which a false idea of fashion had imposed on her!" (ibid., 445).

Parody, like humor, presupposes the truth of the object it caricatures. The transformation of the *Aeneid* into a mock epic is programed, so to speak, by clichés such as "his fear had reached epic proportions." The object of humor, of course, is not Vergil, but the *idée fixe*. Vergil only provides the means to express it, an egregious code for monstrosity. The monstrosity that fiction depicts here is that of anxiety. If humor were attributable to the characters, it would be true enough, since humor is a familiar defensive reaction to the fears we try to repress. Here the narrator is openly responsible for the humor and for its parodic hyperbole, but in using humor for his own purposes (and thus showing his hand), the narrator nonetheless borrows from the characters the discourse of their mental state, of their inner truth.

It remains for me to explain how textual derivations impose upon the reader a symbolism exterior to the narrative. They have to make up for the gap between two discourses and two viewpoints, for the shift from the narrative to its gloss, or to the discourse that gives it its sense or its unity as a work of art. Verisimilitude depends on a fairly uniform sequentiality. It spins a yarn that limits the number of narrative strands to those absolutely required by the need to develop now this and now that character, and to interweave only as many subplots as can be combined without distracting readers and without confusing their perception of simultaneous events and of the order of occurrence of successive ones. This relative simplicity cannot be maintained when symbolism forms pockets of radically different language around which narrative consecution may still be circuitously pursued but whose own mode of expression is alien to consecution itself. Indeed, symbolism has to overcome two obstacles for its truth to impose itself.

The first of these is that the language of the symbolic subtext differs from that of its narrative context to the point that

FICTIONAL TRUTH

it threatens verisimilitude. The symbol rests on an equivalence, on a translation, so to speak, that disproportionately amplifies descriptive details and incidents in the chain of events. The translation develops such details or incidents beyond what the characters can see in them. Their import or their significance is beyond the ken of the characters, because the task of interpreting them is the role reserved for nonparticipants, the readers and the author (or the narrator, as the author's deputy in the text). For the readers and the author, the events of the story are not their own experience, but a text to be decoded. They are in a position to see the tableau after the fact. They can already guess the meaning of the story and conceive of it in its full range. The significance as a whole, moreover, does not depend on the sequence of events but on a retrospective or anticipatory viewpoint. Not only does the truth of the symbol refer to that achronological, instantaneous overview, but it does it through a tropological translation. The trope selected for the translation, for the reference to the story as a whole, serves as a sign that the story, the plot, the fiction is but an example, an illustration of something else, of an ideological telos or simply of an esthetic construct. It signals the change of the story line to make it fit a perspective. The resulting significance is in the perspective, almost in the anamorphosis.

The second obstacle interposed between the symbolic subtext and the story is the very difficulty of translating the latter into the former, of burdening readers with two tasks that are almost incompatible if attempted at the same time. Yet this is precisely what symbolism demands: the decoding of the tale and its overall, atemporal interpretation.

The two problems admit of the same solution: the overdetermination of the verbal sequence. Since the symbolic system translates one discourse into another, using these two discourses to refer to one object, the equivalence between the two—which legitimates the fact that an example is an illustration of something else—must be demonstrated on several levels at once, for instance through homonymy at the phonetic level, synonymy at the semantic level, transformation from word into periphrasis at the syntactic level, etc.

I shall distinguish two kinds of overdetermination, the substitute and the sylleptic type. The first makes the contact between narrative truth, based on verisimilitude, and metalinguistic truth, founded on symbolism, through the mediation of tropes that belong in the verisimilitude system. The second bridges the gap between the two forms of truth, without mediation, by the sole agency of syllepsis. Syllepsis, as we shall see, suffices to bridge the gap between story and commentary, because it is a two-faceted word or phrase equally, although differently, relevant to both discourses, that of verisimilitude and that of metalinguistic symbolism.

My example of substitutive overdetermination is from *The Golden Bowl*. The symbol is the gilded crystal vase of the title. Its function in the narrative is central to the plot, since Maggie Verver discovers the dalliance between the prince, her husband, and her friend Charlotte, when she learns that they had been intimate enough to visit an antique shop together, unbeknownst to her on the eve of her wedding. By herself purchasing the bowl they had thought of buying, she confronts the prince with her discovery. Aside from this narrative function, the bowl is also symbolic. It is symbolic for the characters themselves: they feel (or at least the prince does) that its hidden crack would have made it an ominous gift from Charlotte to Maggie.[7]

Above all, it is symbolic in the eyes of the reader, and this is the particular function of symbolism that is pertinent to fictional truth. The bowl is symbolic for the reader, of course, because Henry James chose the object for his title. Also, and equally important, it is symbolic because the crack in the bowl is already an established sociolectic image for a moral flaw. The description of the object insists on the fact that the crack remains imperceptible beneath the gilding, which makes it even more of an analogy for the deception of which the prince and Charlotte are guilty. This analogy might be only a stylistic ornament, a felicitous parallelism but not necessarily inseparable from the development of the plot.

There is no question, however, that the symbol is insepar-ably fused with the plot, that it is ultimately interiorized, as it were, by the characters themselves. The flawed crystal becomes an image of the prince's inner monologue, of his consciousness, and it dictates the symbolism of his wife's ges-tures when she picks up its pieces, thus declaring her wish to glue her marriage back together. This interiorization by the characters signals the symbol's accession to fictional truth, and, indeed, despite the symbol's being an authorial intru-sion, it serves to confer that truth onto the characters.

The means of that transference from metalanguage to nar-rative, from the author's to the characters' viewpoint, is an *angularity* subtext, in which every mention of an angular item is negated so as to suggest its opposite—smoothness—whether in crystal or in behavior. Developing this model, the novel will be a story of elegant duplicity and of its exposure, as nar-rative spells out the analysis of that smoothness. The subtext is derived from a diegetic given: Mr. Verver's purchase of an Italian prince for his daughter to marry has not been without anxiety that has troubled the quiet father-child intimacy:

> their decent little old-time union, Maggie's and his own, had resembled a good deal some pleasant public square, in the heart of an old city, into which a great Palladian church, say . . . had suddenly been dropped.
>
> (Ibid., chap. 7, 118)

This given expands into a page-long sustained architectural metaphor, concluding that, after all, the Ververs' life has not been made unduly difficult. Air and people circulate freely in and around that intruding monument: "The Palladian church was always there, but the *piazza* took care of itself."

From that given, the subtext's relationship with the narrative develops in three stages: the transforming of the given into the character's own idiolect; pointing the rule for the substitution process; and overdetermination.

In the first stage, Mr. Verver's typical expression, his favorite images (the mimesis of his speech, in the Aristotelian sense of the term, that completes his portrait at the level of verisimilitude) are derived from the church metaphor: indirect free discourse expresses his relief at

> the one prime fact that the Prince, by good fortune, hadn't proved *angular.* He clung to that description of his daughter's husband as he often did to terms and phrases, in the human, the social connexion, that he had found for himself: it was his way to have times of using these constantly, as if they just then lighted the world, or his own path in it, for him — even when for some of his interlocutors they covered less ground. ... [He] came in fact sometimes near publicly pointing the moral of what might have occurred if friction, so to speak, had occurred. He ... mentioned to the Prince the particular justice he did him, was even explicit as to the danger that, in their remarkable relation, they had thus escaped. Oh, if he *had* been *angular!* Who could say what might *then* have happened? He spoke ... as if he grasped the facts, without exception, for which *angularity* stood.
> It figured for him, clearly, as a final idea, a conception of the last vividness. He might have been signifying by it the *sharp corners* and *hard edges*, all the *stony pointedness*, the grand right *geometry* of his spreading Palladian church. Just so, he was insensible to no feature of the felicity of a contract that, beguilingly, almost confoundingly, was a contact but with practically *yielding lines* and *curved surfaces.*[8]

Readers know all along that the church is not the father's image but the narrator's, and that it belongs in a world unknown to Mr. Verver, the metalinguistic commentary out of which all characters are kept: thus the *angularity* lexicon also works as an index of fictionality. As Mr. Verver is carried away by his enthusiasm, new images come to his mind mixing commonplace metaphors and variations on the church image. The latter is now replaced with a Venetian palace, a repression, no doubt, of the narrator's model, and the narrative's way of distancing the mimesis of Mr. Verver's speech from its origins in the narrator's. This next derivation produces as many metonyms of angularity as the previous one:

> 'You're round, my boy,' he had said—'You're *all*, you're variously and inexhaustibly round, when you might, by all the chances, have been abominably square . . . Say you had been formed, all over, in a lot of little pyramidal lozenges like that wonderful side of the Ducal Palace in Venice—so lovely in a building, but so damnable, for rubbing against, in a man, and especially in a near relation. I can see them all from here—each of them sticking out by itself—all the architectural cut diamonds that would have scratched one's softer sides . . . As it is, for living with, you're a pure and perfect crystal. I give you my idea—I think you ought to have it—just as it has come to me.'[9]

The prince, not without cynicism, concurs innerly that "his 'curves' apparently were important because they had been unexpected, or still more, unconceived," and then good-naturedly adopts his father-in-law's last image, thus continuing the process of integrating the narrator's metalanguage into the diegesis: "Oh, if I'm a crystal I'm delighted that I'm a perfect one, for I believe that they sometimes have cracks and flaws."

But in so doing, he enacts the second stage of the linkage between the subtext and the narrative: on the one hand, he adopts a discourse identifying him as smooth; on the other hand, he adapts it to his private knowledge of facts unknown to others, especially his awareness that the one crystal that can be associated with him is indeed flawed. The author's omniscience, an index of fictionality, is here identified with overdetermination, the truth-creating process. This double capability of the character to adopt and adapt posits the equation, the rule of substitution: angularity negated generates smoothness and smoothness now has a name, the Golden Bowl. Hence the predication summarized by that symbol, *smoothness has a flaw*, or better, *this smoothness is really an angularity*, a paradox that now regulates the development of the plot.

The third stage of the transformation that integrates the symbol into the narrative is overdetermination itself, a triple one. It piles up three layers of tropes: first, the discourse of angularity, which is as strongly structured as metonymy, begotten moreover by two striking metaphors (church and palace); second, the transformation of contraries into one another (angularity into smoothness), which packs in one powerful mixture paradox and oxymoron; third, the metaphor that categorizes the prince as an *objet d' art* ("you're a pure and perfect crystal"), developed into a sketch of Mr. Verver as a collector and connoisseur ("no man in Europe or in America, he privately believed, was less capable . . . of vulgar mistakes"). This sketch opens up the tantalizing proairesis of his having made a mistake after all and leads straight to the climax of the plot some thirty chapters later.

Thus is the stage prepared for the suspense of impending exposure: for the *coup de théâtre* that changes the symbol of the prince into a mute witness against him when the bowl is bought by his wife; and for the prolepsis that prophesies the reconciliation of the spouses or Maggie's forbearance when she picks up the pieces of the broken vase and they fit perfectly, suggesting that this Humpty Dumpty can be put together again.

Thus is the truth of the symbol transposed into the truth of the narrative. All that is needed is the addition of the time dimension to the image, or rather to the definition of the word it illustrates, so as to stage successively stories developing the semes of the sememe *crystal* (angularity, smoothness, flaw, breakability) and making their mutual incompatibilities into an epic of conflict, change, and reconciliation.

An objective proof of this interpretation can be found in what we might call the unconscious of the text. A minor flaw in James's phraseology that persists in various forms, the wrong word popping up here and there under the disguise of homonymy, is the revealing ungrammaticality that allows us to verify a consecution that has nothing to do with the narrative chain of acts and their consequences. It has everything to do with the unchanging, obsessive presence of *angularity*, angularity itself or angularity in its complementary form, the flawed smoothness of the Prince—flawed because he remains in fact secretly angular, inassimilable by the original happy couple.

The "flaw" is James's making Mr. Verver use *square* to speak of the angularity he had feared in the prince, a fear that he mistakenly and too hastily dismissed as unfounded: "You're *all*, you're variously and inexhaustibly round, when you might, by all the chances, have been abominably square." Whereas *round* is an accepted colloquialism to denote a straightforward honesty in speech and demeanor, as well as "free from angularity" when speaking of a person (this is verbatim the revealing complementarity of the *Oxford English Dictionary*'s definition), *square* is not its natural, grammatical opposite (in fact, the adjective's connotations are nowise negative). The reason for James's choosing it nevertheless must be found not in language but in the repression of the actual generator of the symbol: *square* approximates, on the one hand, in "body language," in personality, the angularity presupposed by *round*. On the other hand, it echoes the *square*, the little "Verver piazza" symbolic of domestic bliss, that is suddenly invaded, occupied, in the significantly bizarre initial metaphor, by the falling into it, as a meteorite from a cloudless sky, of the prince's Palladian and angular church: a stone in the Ververs' garden, a violation of the father-daughter *ménage*. It is quite clear that this invasion is echoed by the prince's first name, Amerigo, a veritable play on America Italianized.[10] And whereas *round* corrects the square rival into a smooth son-in-law, the translation of his roundness into that of a flawed crystal negativizes again the smooth prince into a lurking "smoothie."

It is therefore the more remarkable that the avatars of squareness culminate in a last *square* that cancels out the initial one four hundred pages later, thus closing the angularity subtext. This last variant is brought about most artificially and thus the more revealingly by the astonishing scruples (James's stated surprise) of the antique dealer who insists on returning the money paid for the bowl by the injured wife for three revealingly "bad" reasons. The little shopman unaccountably insists that he is impelled to do so because he "likes" her, whereas he had not "liked" Amerigo; because he does not want the bowl to bring ill luck to her father ("the flaw . . . would make it, verily, as an offering to a loved parent, a thing of sinister meaning and evil effect"); and because, if he did not avert the danger and reveal the flaw, he would not have "been quite 'square' over their little business" (ibid., chap. 35, 450–52; James's emphasis!). The same word thus generates the *angularity* sequence and its positive (but fallaciously so) corollary, the *smoothness* sequence. Truth prevails, this time symbolized by the imperative of language, when the same word represents through its homonymic variants the good and the bad, when, like Achilles's spear that alone could cure the wounds it inflicted, *square* signals the beginning of the drama—a story of happy incest invaded by an interloper—and its end, love victorious and legitimacy redeemed, the prince forgiven, the father exiled, and everything squarely, or roundly, back into place. The whole narrative comes to a happy conclusion, back to square one.

The second type of overdetermination that makes words into a symbolic metalanguage of the fictional text is sylleptic. Syllepsis is, of course, the trope that consists in the simultaneous presence of two meanings for one word. It is not to be confused with ambiguity, in which two (or more) meanings are proffered, between which we are at a loss to choose. Syllepsis, on the contrary, forces us not to choose, compelling us to recognize the equal necessity and equal actualization of both alternatives. Text generation solves this conundrum by actualizing at the lexical level, in a single word, the meaning compatible with the context preceding the syllepsis, and by actualizing the other meaning, the one incompatible with that context, in the form of periphrases that are clearly equivalent to the sylleptic word and that derive from it sometimes after an interval. Typically, the trope posits a parallelism, an equation between two readings of the same symbolic character, situation, or event: one is the mimetic reading, one the hermeneutic; or, one is the supposedly objective version, one the version from a specific viewpoint such as the narrator's.

Such is the generative process in what I will call the *Bois de Boulogne* subtext in Proust. The *Bois*, of course, is to Paris what Central Park is to New York, and in the period depicted in *A la Recherche du temps perdu*, it was in its tree-shaded drives that the beautiful people displayed themselves and vied with each other in elegant horse-drawn carriages. There, expensive, kept women, but also society women on the prowl, would parade their beauty. And there the narrator was taken as a child and watched Odette Swann drive by, the most seductive of them all, femininity itself, and, because of her celebrated misconduct, the paragon of objects of desire. Finally, it is there that as a grown man he returns to remember and find the beautiful women gone, but Beauty itself lingering in his memory where the fantastic park, the park of his fancy, cannot be erased by the real park.

First, the poetic given is posited. The imaginary interpretation, without which the narrative would merely be a cheap recording of social habits, is the decision (itself motivated, from beyond the literary horizon by the universal law of the libido) to see and therefore to describe a woman as a masterpiece. This imaginary axiom is phrased similarly to the apodeictic statements described in the first chapter:

> Thinking that Beauty—in the order of feminine elegance—was governed by occult laws into the knowledge of which they had been initiated, and that they had the power to realise it, I accepted in advance like a revelation the appearance of their clothes, of their carriages and horses, of countless details in which I placed my faith as in an inner soul which gave the cohesion of a work of art to that ephemeral and shifting pageant. But it was Mme Swann whom I wished to see.[11]

In a second step, one that is properly narrative, the given's defining feature, that is, that art is immortal, is realized through one more instance of Time immobilized or suspended by memory. This is achieved by the narrator's rereading of the text in which Beauty once manifested herself in a female passerby. This text is the park itself, now revisited. Or rather, it is the narrative of the lady remembered as being driven through the park, with attendant details such as gazes exchanged with gentlemen, stepping out of the carriage to walk followed by them, etc., all of these incidents being so many indices of admiration and therefore renewed demonstrations of her beauty. Verisimilitude demands that witnesses be distributed along the road, their admiring unanimity thus transforming into a tautological narrative the axiomatic identification of the passing Odette Swann with unchanging Beauty, the equation posited in two words by the given.

But this second step, being diegetic and no longer apodeictic, could fail to enlist readers' agreement or the acceptance that they could not deny to the apodeictic given. The burden of proof is now shifted to a syllepsis. Passing beauty could be permanent beauty if Time were rooted to a spot, if the Bois de Boulogne were thus the ideal chronotope. This is indeed what a syllepsis achieves by the most simplistic of puns. It is brought about by a sentence that is also apodeictic (the narrator simply says it is the way he feels about the park) but that ends in a phrase that presupposes the pun:

> the Bois de Boulogne was to me like one of those zoological gardens in which one sees assembled together a variety of flora and contrasted landscapes, where from a hill one passes to a grotto, a meadow, rocks, a stream, a pit, another hill, a marsh, but knows that they are there only to enable the hippopotamus, zebra, crocodile, rabbit, bear and heron to disport themselves in a natural or a picturesque setting; it, the Bois, equally complex, uniting a multitude of little worlds, distinct and separate—alternating a plantation of redwood trees and American oaks, like an experimental forest in Virginia, with a fir-wood by the edge of the lake, or a grove from which would suddenly emerge, in her raiment of soft fur, with the large, appealing eyes of a dumb animal, a hastening walker—was the Garden of Women; and like the myrtle alley in the *Aeneid*, planted for their delight with trees of one kind only, the Allée des Acacias was thronged with the famous beauties of the day.[12]

The phrase *the Garden of Women*, especially in the context of a zoological and botanical garden, cannot avoid recalling for the French the principal garden that happens to be both zoological and botanical, the *Jardin des Plantes* in Paris. Despite the trite appearance of the phrase, it is the only one of its kind in French, with one exception, *Jardin des Femmes*, which the novel has just coined (and, to be complete, *Jardin des Supplices*, the title of a novel by Octave Mirbeau, but this last farfetched variant suggests how little productive this phrase pattern is). No reader can avoid this reference in a novel that time and again alludes to the latent equation of the feminine and the floral: first, through the title of the second volume, *A l'Ombre des jeunes filles en fleurs*; second, by insistently describing women as gracious plants with flexible stems (Proust even coins a compound noun for them: *les filles fleurs*, "the flower-like girls"); third, by having a special subtext starting before the passage in question and continuing long after it, in which a young man, himself an object of desire, is described as arborescent and then metamorphosed into a human sapling (*arbuste humain*); fourth, by spelling out the equivalence in the words of no less than the Baron de Charlus, the theorist of desire as an art form and the most important character after the narrator. Charlus describes his ideal of love as one of possession, an ideal the reader can hardly ignore since the novel will include a volume entitled *La Prisonnière* ("The Love Captive"):

> Gardening is an alibi ... We cultivate begonias, we trim yew trees ... because yew trees and begonias let us do what we like with them. But we should prefer to spend our time on a human tree (*arbuste humain*).[13]

Such is the unthinkable paradox, but one grammatically correct, guaranteed and supported, as it were, by the double face of the phrase *Jardin des Plantes/Jardin des Femmes*, an impossibility that has become so possible verbally that it now generates the subtext. However, a mimesis grounded in verisimilitude has limitations. These allow for only three possible solutions, all three tested in turn by the derivative sequence. One narrative solution is to fill the park with desirable women. But this also has a revealing twist: the narrator goes so far as to say that there are paths reserved for such women, to wit:

> like the myrtle-alley in Vergil's *Aeneid*, planted for their delight with trees of one kind only, the Allée des Acacias . . . thronged with the famous beauties of the day, [and] the Allée de la Reine-Marguerite, where women went who wanted to be alone, or to appear to want to be alone.[14]

The second solution is mimetically figurative: it consists in describing trees as if they were women. This is the case for the acacias, which with their "coquettish outline, the delicate fabric of their lightly tossing foliage, its easy grace, . . . and finally their name itself, feminine, indolent, dulcet, made my heart beat."[15] The third solution is the one that language provides whenever something must be depicted that transcends or crosses natural barriers between the three reigns of Nature: namely, the fantastic genre and its mythological or supernatural representations. Mythological:

> The trees forced for so many years now, by a sort of grafting process, to share in the life of feminine humanity, . . . called to my mind the figure of the dryad [tree nymph] . . . swiftly walking, brightly coloured, whom they shelter with their branches as she passes beneath them, obliging her to acknowledge as they themselves do, the power of the season.[16]

As for the supernatural or fantastic mimesis, Odette Swann's carriage horses and her carriage are described as an apparition, a chariot traveling through the sky:

Those horses, frenzied and light as wasps on the wing, with bloodshot eyes like the cruel steeds of Diomed, which now, smitten by a desire to see again what I had once loved, as ardent as the desire that had driven me many years before along the same paths, I wished to see anew before my eyes at the moment when Mme Swann's enormous coachman, supervised by a groom no bigger than his fist and as infantile as St. George in the picture, endeavoured to curb the ardour of the quivering steel-tipped pinions with which they thundered over the ground.[17]

This image itself is a literal derivation from a commonplace metaphor when speaking of fast horses (they seem to fly):

borne along by the flight of a pair of fiery horses, slender and shapely as one sees them in the drawings of Constantin Guys [the chronicler of Parisian society life celebrated by Baudelaire].[18]

Such are the images with which the narrator modifies the basic elements of an objective mimesis of the Bois de Boulogne, one readers could either have recognized (if they knew the place) or found acceptable (if they had only verisimilitude to help them on). He rewrites the Bois of memory into today's walks and thus stays the flight of Time. The clausula consists in undoing that undoing, and the subtext, therefore, ends with a return to objective prose mimesis: the heavenly chariot is no longer to be seen, replaced as it has been with modern automobiles. The park no longer resembles the women it had represented (in tree or vegetation codes), hence, the following tautological or rather circular similes, from like to like, which would be nonsensical if they did not signal the return to the point of departure where an embedding for a moment swelled out the narrative:

The sun had gone. Nature was resuming its reign over the Bois, from which had vanished all trace of the idea that it was the Elysian Garden of Woman; above the gimcrack windmill the real sky was grey; the wind wrinkled the surface of the Grand Lac in little wavelets, like a real lake; large birds flew swiftly over the Bois, as over a real wood.[19]

In using intertextuality and syllepsis as the mainstays of the interpretive process, I have been describing twofold symbolizing processes. Significance cannot be produced without first voiding, displacing, or repressing an established meaning, whether this meaning originates in the sociolect or in the context. This, of course, is similar or identical to the workings of the unconscious. I propose to explore this parallelism between the psychological and the textual unconscious in the next chapter, and thus to restitute some substance to the fictional truth that I have so far described as a function.

Four

The Unconscious of Fiction

The various instances of truth in fiction that I have examined so far have in common a basis of well-defined and necessarily perceived formal features. All of them are either distinct from verisimilitude or exclude it altogether, since all of them are compatible with indices of fictionality. Moreover, although verisimilitude presupposes things, concepts, or sign systems against which the text may be tested for accuracy and evaluated in the light of their authority, fictional truth spurns referentiality that raises the specter of whether or not the reader acknowledges its accuracy. Instead, fictional truth relies entirely on the text itself as if the latter were self-sufficient. Truth is a modality of text generation. Several possibilities can therefore be distinguished. First, truth may issue from textual transformations of a given, regulated by the mechanisms of continuous semiosis and formal substitutability, the latter being a generalization of the principle that underlies rhetoric, namely, that any trope or figure can be perceived and defined only so long as it presupposes another expression for which it is a substitute. Second, truth is inferred from apodeictic discourse, from predications framed in axiomatic formulas. Third, truth is inferred from the tautological verification of a lexical or phrasal given by the text it generates: in this case, truth is derivative, idiolectic, paradigmatic, and, eventually, circular. Fourth, truth is represented by symbols, themselves developed into subtexts, whose sign systems comment on the narrative and repeat its elements in a different form, thus presupposing the reality of what it glosses. In all four categories, veridictory discourse is outside of and parallel to the narrative, a metalanguage of it, and therefore rests entirely on the logical imperatives of presupposition and entailment.

As we now turn to the unconscious of fiction, it would seem that we have yet another instance of presupposition. It is common wisdom that the unconscious harbors in symbolic and cryptic form a truth that we repress at the conscious level. The unconscious is therefore assumed to stand in regard to consciousness as does reality in regard to appearances. Consequently, whenever the text seems to hide something, that something is supposed to be true. But, of course, when we say that the text seems to conceal or to screen instead of telling and showing, we actually mean that there are in the text formal indices suggesting that the words of that text have another face, that they could easily be interpreted otherwise, or explained by motivations other than those appropriate to the story as told and the situation as described. This is on the model of the psychological unconscious, which we assume contains meanings that describe our real selves but that are inappropriate to public consumption or imply other than socially acceptable verbal or material behavior. I shall try to show that these assumptions are either loose talk, or simply irrelevant extrapolation from the psychological to the textual unconscious.

The unconscious of a text cannot be floating in limbo in the sociolect or in the reader's mind (probably two ways of saying the same thing). It has to be intertextual, the intertext being the analogon or reverse face of the text and thus a text or series of texts selected as referents by the text we are reading. Furthermore, this intertext must be identifiable from elements of the verbal sequence we are trying to interpret, or at least its probable location must be indicated. The intertext is hidden like the psychological unconscious and, like that unconscious, it is hidden in such a way that we cannot help finding it.

I submit that readers experience this discovery or recovery of the hidden, and therefore perform an exercise of truth-finding in two possible ways: by comparative reading and by double-take. Double-take is the perception of syllepsis. By comparative reading, I mean the reader's empirical perception of structures. As readers progress through one or more novels, they come to realize that apparently unconnected and diverse representations or stories have relational and functional features in common that direct interpretation beyond what each instance authorizes. Therefore, these several representations and stories are now recognized as variants of structural invariants. The significance common to a set of variants, the significance readers can deduce from invariance, supersedes the separate meanings that the variants have when read in isolation. This significance thus has the permanence, the generality, and the freedom from contingence that we associate with truth.

One such invariant is the literary representation of desire. This structure applies to desire in its broadest sense, the craving for any object whose possession is deemed worthy by the subject. For desire to exist subjects must project their libidos onto the object and the predication expressing this projection must be negated or postponed. Otherwise, fulfillment would be attained and desire would cease to exist. The structure of desire must accordingly be comprised of a desiring subject and an object both attractive and frustrating. The latter is therefore usually represented as frightening or repellent as well as desirable, or out of reach, either absent or separated from the subject by actual or imaginary obstacles. Hence the kinship between desire and narrative; it might even be possible to postulate a hierarchy that would subordinate narrative structures proper to an overarching libidinal structural system (every device postponing a *dénouement*, for instance, or heightening suspense, every hurdle slowing the protagonist's quest at once fosters desire and lengthens the narrative). Even though desire applies to everything, sexual desire is especially germane to the unconscious, since it is the form of desire most likely to be repressed.

A rather hot example of fictional desire is to be found in one of Victor Hugo's most bizarre and fascinating novels, *L'Homme qui rit* (*The Laughing Man*), a melodramatic story set in seventeenth-century England. The melodrama taxes credibility and Hugo's England is quite improbable, yet the novel is realistic enough to give us the feeling that a whole period of history has come to life. Poetic truth takes over and challenges every rule of verisimilitude, as well as the conventions of the historical novel. Yet the feelings and thoughts Hugo puts into the characters caught in this most unlikely of plots breathe truth nonetheless, and they explicitly embody impulses that would not be analyzed until Freud half a century later. The protagonist is a young man who was kidnapped by gypsies, whose face has been disfigured in such a way that he seems to be always laughing. This is how he makes a living, as an artificial monster for the amusement of the crowds. The face, however, tops a promising body, and he attracts an idle, bored, sexually frustrated young lady who occasionally goes slumming. She throws herself at him, which exemplifies a motif of male fantasies that moralists have harped upon from the Greek satirists and Juvenal in Rome down through modern times. Her sister, the queen, a model of the bad queen intent on ensnaring the heroine in the web of her lust, has the young man plucked from the gutter and locked in a labyrinth of splendid apartments in the Duchess Josiane's palace, at the end of which maze he finds the royal hysteric he has been fantasizing about asleep, naked, and defenseless in her boudoir. She is, says Hugo, "his evil thoughts made living flesh."[1] Aside from the unlikely plot, there is nothing in the scene that strains psychological verisimilitude. With a change of setting, garb, and social relations, we would have a most convincing scene of erotic voyeurism that could have come from the pen of D. H. Lawrence or even Henry Miller. Moreover, every narrative detail is exemplary and meant to heighten tension. Her déshabillé is a diaphanous clinging nightdress. In her lurid slumber, she has the suggestive position of the agitated sleeping beauty in Fuseli's famous painting *The Nightmare*:

> She was sleeping with her head hanging low over the bedside, one foot pushing away the blanket, like the succubus above whom a dream beats its wings.[2]

The reader is led to suppose that she is dreaming of the very man who is now watching her—an exciting circularity.

Although, as I have said, verisimilitude is hardly affected by the implausible locale and the incredible social circumstances, as long as the diegesis remains convincing, I am not referring only to a psychological motivation that would be valid anywhere anytime, but rather to its exemplarity, the litmus test of truth. This exemplarity, however, does not consist merely in the derivative tautology about which I invoked

Lewis Carroll's authority (*What I say three times is true*). It consists in the polarity of the relationships between actors. I do not mean just the polarity that brings their emotions to a fever pitch (as it actually does) nor a genre-induced polarity (the genre in this case being melodrama). I mean the polarity that focuses readers' attention on the syntax of the desire predication, which is so starkly oppositional that it is a geometry as much as it is a syntax, on verbal logic, as it were, translating into words the dynamics of an arrested psychological impulse, on the very grammar of language.

Focusing is achieved in four stages: first, in the apparent paradox—"he realized that what he was seeing was a fearsome thing, a naked woman"[3]; second, in the descriptive oxymoron combining lust and suspense—"Between her nakedness and his gaze, there were two obstacles, her nightdress and the gauze curtain, two transparencies"[4]; then an abstract translation into conventional symbols, this time in the narrator's voice—"Was she a whore? Was she a virgin? Messalina, perhaps invisibly present, was surely smiling. Diana was surely standing guard. Her beauty had the lure of inaccessibility"[5]; and as an introduction to all this and a corrective for the dated philosophical bombast—a bathtub of black marble before the bed. It is black, says Hugo, to change the whiteness of her flesh into splendor.[6] It is empty, which makes it the symbol *a contrario* of the fair bather that it will no doubt soon display. Similarly, in bucolic settings, it is a literary cliché to describe an isolated pond or natural spring in the forest as Diana's bath, and to stress its emptiness so that it is better described as full of her latent presence. To top all this off, from Josiane's marble bath, an elegant jet of water spouts up, looking like a "flexible steel rod" (*une souple verge d'acier* [ibid., 421], with the aggravating circumstance that steel points to something other than water and that *verge*, a sophisticated literary word for "rod," is also a very graphic common term for "penis").

This symbolism is of course self-evident, and yet the reader's obvious interpretation is disturbed by aberrant features. First, the Duchess Josiane is at once repulsive and attractive, as if the dialectical structure were interiorized by her instead of being, as usual, spread along the narrative: her eyes are not of the same color, one blue and one black, "heavenly eye, hellish eye" (ibid., 428; cf. 178), as Hugo puts it. Furthermore, she looks as if she were swimming in her sleep: *She was moving softly on the bed, undulating, composing and decomposing fascinating curves. Her body had the litheness of water.*[7] This watery nature specifically represents the monster in her: once awakened, garrulous and pedantic, she so informs her visitor, calling herself *Amphitrite fluctivoma*, the sea goddess vomiting water. She says to the poor fellow: *You bring out my true nature. Your being so close makes the hydra in me come out.*[8] "Hydra," the monster's name, means "water."

All this would be gibberish if so many ungrammaticalities did not cause readers to make the connection with another of Hugo's novels where these anomalies make sense, and in the context of which they are grammatical: one cannot help remembering the most famous scene in *Les Travailleurs de la mer* (*The Labourers of the Sea*), the encounter between a sailor stranded on a reef and an octopus. The protagonist first sights the monster, a real hydra and not a mythological figment, in a sea cave at low tide. In that cave, alternately described as the palace of Death himself and as a shrine, there is a rock that resembles an altar or a pedestal, but it is empty of its idol. Applying the same metonymic rule as for Josiane's bath, Hugo describes this emptiness as the proof first of a recent presence: *a naked woman probably was on that altar a moment ago.*[9] Then he translates this absence into a latent presence: it must be *a statue of the Ideal* (ibid.), of a Diana, he adds, but one who could bring herself to love. At that very moment, the octopus appears swimming next to the altar, less the antithesis than the corollary of desire, and described as a chimera, which puts it on the same mythological level as the Ideal personified. As Duchess Josiane says in her text of which this is the intertext, *the monstrous* (literally, *deformity) is the other face of the sublime.*[10]

One more invariant of the structure must be underscored. It prepares with appropriate suspense the *coup de théâtre* of finding oneself in the presence of beauty and horror rolled into one: it is the maze that leads as a tortuous initiation to the discovery. The sailor arrives at the cave after a painful slithering through rocky crevices and narrow galleries. The laughing man similarly has to go through a labyrinth of luxurious chambers now paradoxically and therefore pointedly described as the holes of a madrepore. The sailor discovers an "extraordinary cave,"[11] the laughing man only "penetrates the unexpected,"[12] but that unexpected, the duchess's boudoir, is said to be a "grotto of mirrors" (ibid.). This is not, or not only, because it is furnished like a bordello, but because the cave, imported from the intertext and now high and dry, has to replace watery reflections with shimmering glass.

It should be clear by now that the intertext of the narrative acts as the unconscious of fiction and that readers recover or discover that intertext because the narrative itself contains clues leading back to it. This is in no way different from the process that leads the analyst from anomalies, inconsequences, and non sequiturs in the analysand's monologue to a key to the latter's symbols and symptoms. It must also be clear that the narrative is produced by repressing and displacing the intertext, and that the visible sign of this repression or displacement at the surface of the fictional text is the loss of narrativity. In *Les Travailleurs de la mer*, the complementarity of the sublime and the horrible is the hyperbolic form of the telos of the protagonist's actual quest through the rocks of the reef (he is looking for food, for shells and fish). Because of the successivity of events, this complementarity still has to be represented by distributing both components in the frame of a chronotope (the octopus is there, the statue of the Ideal is gone). In *L'Homme qui rit*, on the contrary, the intertext surfaces only through a metaphor, which enables one character to fuse both components into one, the metaphor being alternately in the narrator's discourse and in the character's consciousness of her inner conflicts and the ensuing hysterical logorrhea.

Once the intertext is in the background, its productivity ceases only with the end of the author's corpus, following the progress that we have already observed in the case of subtexts, whose idiolectic idiosyncrasies increased as they repeated themselves further and further away from the given. Whereas this given is the sociolect in the case of the subtext, it is the intertext in the case of the diegetic variants of a structure.

This is why the following amorous encounter in Hugo's greatest novel, *Les Misérables*, between a naive young man and a blossoming maiden, is ridiculous bathos and near nonsense unless the octopus is perceived within the girl, however innocent, sheltered, and candid this hardly nubile child may be. They exchange their first timid glance of recognition in a public garden. Everything is nice around them, ideal and simon-pure. And yet, as she steals a furtive glance at him:

> It was a strange bolt of lightning . . . What he had just seen was not the ingenuous and simple gaze of a child. It was a mysterious chasm opening only to close again suddenly. There always comes a day when a young woman casts such a look. Woe to whoever happens to be there.[13]

In the same way that the imaginary statue and the octopus, separate in the intertext, were fused in one woman in the corresponding text, the next novel, using the previous one as its intertext, fuses that woman's varicolored eyes into one gaze:

Purity and burning passion are combined in this celestial and fatal ray of light ... It has the magic power, stronger than the most artful glance of a coquette, of making a dark flower bloom, full of odor and poison, that is called love.[14]

Three chapters later, as the two adolescents, taking the next faltering step in their innocent flirtation, look into each other's eyes, the text explodes into a mad, obsessive imagery that would be sheer nonsense if we did not recognize in it, organizing it, the ghost outline of the octopus intertext:

A woman's gaze resembles certain machines, apparently motionless and yet formidable. We pass by with impunity, without suspecting anything. The time comes when we even forget that this thing is near us. ... Then all of a sudden we feel we are caught. It is all over. The machine holds you tight, the gaze has caught you ... You are lost. You will be swallowed whole ... You fight in vain. No human help can save you. You are going to fall from gearwheel to gearwheel, from one anguish to the next, from one torture to another, you, your mind, your fortune, your future, your soul ... and you will escape that frightening machinery either disfigured by shame or transfigured by passion.[15]

To be sure, the image is that of cogs and wheels, but the sequence is digestive, if I may say, and there is also, incidentally, a parallelism with Hugo's sadistic depiction of a human prey of the octopus, emptied into the monster's inner void, digested alive, pumped in by the animated pneumatic machine to which he fancies the suction cups of the tentacles are hooked. Their sudden grip on one's limb is the most celebrated quotation from the octopus episode, a moment selected for a dramatic picture in illustrated editions of *Travailleurs de la mer*. Again, the water has run out, but it was needed only for the verisimilitude of the beast, since there is no such thing as a *terra firma* cephalopod, except of course in the fantasies of our fears and the mythology that has enshrined them in literature. Freud has taught us to recognize in this a more pointed symbol of one's sexual desire and anxiety, the Medusa's head. But even without Freud's help, we would have known, for a literary text always has its own key to unlock the unconscious. Hugo, first to introduce that octopus into literature, depicted it as "Medusa with eight snakes to serve her every whim."[16]

The best evidence for the incidental nature of the role played by the sea and for the fact that the octopus itself is simply an image for a deeper structure of the unconscious is that both sea and sea monster may disappear from some variants, so long as the function or mechanism of the monster remains represented, however abstractly. In *Les Misérables*, the underground flight of the protagonist through the sewers of Paris is one such variant. Desire here is for the light at the end of the tunnel, the open, freedom for Jean Valjean and the wounded barricade fighter he is carrying away from the street battle toward life and toward his stepchild, Cosette, our virgin octopus of the previous quotation, the wounded man being the adolescent she had made eyes at. As for the interdicting structure, since there are no scuttlefish in sewage, the monster's function is divided into two symbols. The symbol for the obstacle, the fearful suspense before fulfillment, is distributed equally among: first, the setting (the iron gate at the mouth of the sewer that seems at first to negate any hope); second, a negative character (the gangster who has a key, but opens the gate only in the hope of delivering Valjean into the hands of the waiting police outside); and third, a positive character (the policeman, who changes his mind and lets Valjean go, thus providing a miracle, desire fulfilled, because the novel still has some mileage to run, or rather, because in the stations of the protagonist's passion or of his progress from crime to sainthood—the theme of the novel—a higher rung of desire has to be proffered for him to be entirely purged of sin). As for the picturesque of the monster, its verisimilitude, its narrative motivation—the viscous swallowing and ignoble suction—it is displaced onto the labyrinth itself and represented by the last peril or trap before deliverance, the quicksand that nearly swallows up Jean Valjean.

It is at this point of reading that a new condensation of symbols (in the sense of Freud's *Verdichtung*) takes place: it is the labyrinth that has become the monster, a monster whose monstrosity is the abject, abjection itself, since it now has intestinal features. There is nothing surprising here since, on the one hand, the octopus's deadly suction had been described in excremental terms: "Glued, tied up, powerless, you feel slowly emptied into that awful bag, the monster"[17]; and on the other hand, the title of the chapters in which the protagonist is caught in the sewers gives them a metaphorical name that is also the interpretation of their symbolism: *The Bowels of Leviathan*. There is a final overturning of the significance, the appearance of the other face of horror and abjection, that is, fulfillment. The same swallowing up by the octopus lends itself to a switch from symbolic discourse back to the mimesis of intercourse: "The octopus's suction cup is you yourself penetrating the beast."[18]

Not every recovery of the intertext requires the comparative procedure, extended to a complex corpus, that I have described so far. Comparative reading is the rule when one reads an author throughout or when one perceives novels as belonging to a genre. The genre then regulates and directs comparisons as if it were a multi-author corpus. Within one work of fiction, the same approach may be dictated by the presence of cognate subtexts. If these are lacking, readers have to perform an analysis that is guided and programed by the semantic features of the given from which a narrative sequence issues.

We must not confuse the unconscious of fiction with the

unconscious of the author or of the reader. The latter is accessible to psychoanalysis, the former to semanalysis. At any rate, even though the unconscious as we experience it prompts the genesis of texts that, in turn, have an intertextual unconscious, what explains the genesis of narrative is irrelevant to what explains its production, that is, its reading, its hermeneutic actualization by the reader. One of the most widespread subtexts in Marcel Proust's huge novel is the *undersea* or *underwater* subtext, that can more precisely be called the *aquarium wall* subtext, whose function is to develop metaphorically the significance of snobbishness and social exclusion. This is, of course, along with the immobilization of time and with homosexuality, one of the three main strands of the novel's fabric.

Social exclusion and the yearning to be admitted within circles from which one has been kept out is not the dated concern some critics believe it to be, irrelevant to readers of the present and of the future (this is assuming that snobbishness is not as central to today's society as it was in Proust's time, which I do not believe for a minute). It is not dated because whatever mimetic relevance it may have had for Proust's contemporaries, it remains alive and functional as a trope, as a stylistic variant for the structure of desire and its corollary interdiction, now transferred from the sexual to the social libido.

The subtext's initial fully developed version occurs in the ten-page story of a benefit evening at the opera. Subscribers' boxes have been reserved for members of the Princesse de Guermantes's party, the most exclusive group in Paris. Less extraordinary spectators, who fill the orchestra seats, are more interested in watching the Guermantes crowd than in following the spectacle on stage. The barrier separating the two worlds is an invisible one; this the reader deduces from the description of the boxes as submarine caves, of the dimly lit house in terms of the swimming chiaroscuro of the briny deep, of male spectators as Tritons, and of their décolletéed ladies as half-naked sea nymphs. All this can be seen but not touched, let alone entered, as if an aquarium's window separated the two worlds. The description translates into mimetic terms the grammar of desire: a frustrated craving for progress from one sensory perception to full sensual possession. This imagery developed long before the advent of the aquarium or of plate glass, with Latin poetry from Vergil to Catullus depicting sea goddesses in their sea caves, visible under water, a temptation to the sentimental angler but beyond the reach of mere mortals.

Thus, in the "Night at the Opera" passage, the central image of another world seen through the transparency of water but out of the reach of land-bound creatures is duplicated in the eyes of the ladies of that inaccessible society, as if these eyes were themselves parts of an aquarium's plate glass wall:

> Beyond began the orchestra stalls, abode of mortals for ever separated from the sombre and transparent realm to which here and there, in their smooth liquid surface, the limpid, reflecting eyes of the water-goddesses served as frontier. For the folding seats on its shore and the forms of the monsters in the stalls were mirrored in those eyes in simple obedience to the laws of optics and according to their angle of incidence, as happens with those two sections of external reality to which, knowing that they do not possess any soul, however rudimentary, that can be considered analogous to our own, we should think ourselves insane to address a smile or a glance: namely, minerals and people to whom we have not been introduced.[19]

Elsewhere one can see the monocle of an aristocrat, insignia of snobbery, from behind which peers a pleasant but condescending eye: "His gaze [is] a disc of rock crystal" (ibid., 2:40; 2:36). In other variants, absurdity stems from analogy:

the derivative idiolect singles out and valorizes any barrier or limit that, like the plate glass, is physically flimsy but remains morally unbreakable.

> While the rich young man's friends envied him because he had such a smartly dressed mistress, the latter's scarves hung before the little company a sort of fragrant, flowing veil, but one that kept it apart from the outer world.[20]

These images, whether or not authorized by the figurative, are unacceptable and, as a result, readers cannot forget them. Since they keep exemplifying libidinal dynamics, this coincidence makes the unacceptable a hyperbolic form of the illustrative. Finally, the semiosis incorporates representations incompatible with the given. A doormat at the door of a duke represents a border that excludes people one does not receive: beyond that doormat fantasy conjures up minarets, mosques, and palm trees (cf. ibid., vol. 2:30, 542; 2:25; 563).

Without the "Night at the Opera" version, we could not make sense of monocles described as fragments of the plate glass of an aquarium window nor of eyes depicted as translucent barriers, nor could we understand Proust's partiality to glass enclosures through which the have-nots watch the haves, and we would find it nonsensical that a doormat, the pedestrian symbol of acceptance, should give onto an inaccessible luscious exoticism.

We have seen how the paradigms of repetition peter out as they unfold, losing more and more of their mimetic components, becoming progressively more allusive until textuality itself vanishes and the final allusions are reduced to an isolated word or phrase. An idiolect thus develops with rules that have been given once, in the subtext's first version, often at a great distance from the point readers have reached. A whole construction, its rules, its difference, its ability to do without the help of the sociolect, or to do away with it, can now be evoked by one word in which the subtext's features are concentrated. It is as if the text had returned from the written to the entirely unwritten. Its own interpretation, plus a collection of examples destined to prove the point, plus a system of signs meant to help readers perceive the work of art as a unified, harmonious whole—all this that gives the text its identity and its fullest artistic development is now as though committed back to memory, as though the telos of the literary text were to spell out a story only as a rehearsal for an imaginary mnemonic possession of it.

I am not just referring to our ability to remember a book we have read; that would amount to belaboring the obvious. I am referring to the mechanism that has enabled the text to build within its fabric pockets of implicitly remembered, symbolic stories in which its essence is resumed and whose sole purpose is to store up indices of its significance, mementos of its important points, guidelines for the easy control of an understanding of its fully developed complex. These traveler's aids all have their key, the word from which the subtext can be reconstituted whole (just as the text can be inferred from the subtexts), and this key, this word itself, is identifiable because it recalls the initial wording of the subtext's first instance. In other words, the literariness of the written text is built on a circularity of memory.

But what about the beginnings of the subtexts? What about the beginning of the text? The answer is probably that memory, too, is responsible for the first valorization of a lexical or phrasal representation, making it capable of simultaneously carving out an intertext and generating a textual derivation as a consequence of intertextual input. Since this memory is the original one, it is also an unconscious one, and one may well wonder how readers can have access to it and experience its motivational power, the ultimate authority for the truth of the text. The answer, I think, lies in that symbol of the text's limits, the quotation, or the allusion, which is also, as the fragment that it is, *the* sign whose special function is to stand for memory.

In the aquarium wall example, the unconscious memory that imparts to the subtext the full dynamics of the libido by giving underwater imagery the primary role is eighteen pages into the three thousand-page novel, an apparently quite far-fetched allusion to the story of Aristaeus in Vergil's *Georgics*. This mythological hero was the inventor of apiculture. Having problems raising bees, he is said to have gone for advice into the underwater kingdom of his mother, the nymph Cyrene. Vergil shows him crying for help at the lip of the chasm opening onto the depths, heard by the nymph and her retinue of marine deities, and received, full of admiration for his mother's watery empire (*umida regna*[21]). This story has furnished Proust with the setting for his subtext, and the exclusion principle is repeatedly emphasized by the Latin source. A revealing slip of the pen suggests what Proust's motivation in making so much of the story must have been. Proust substitutes Tethys, a much better known sea goddess, often written about since Homer, for Vergil's nymph. Proust makes a further mistake, however, and replaces Tethys with Thetis, a lesser sea goddess who was the mother of Achilles. Twice shying before the name, this graphemic stuttering is readily spotted by readers of the post-Freudian era.

I suspect that Thetis was mistakenly substituted for Cyrene because Proust's problem was his fear of maternal rejection. The first pages of *La Recherche* are about nothing else. The child's anxiety at not having his mother come to kiss him goodnight, the jealousy towards the father, all of this is obvious and informs the whole novel. Vergil's text, standard at the time in Latin classes, must have riveted Proust's attention at school, because Aristaeus is anxious, because when he asks for his mother's help, he is shut out of her intimate circle of attractive nymphs exactly as the narrator as a child will be from the family circle, because his anxiety manifests itself by a hint at family romance (*Was my father Apollo, as you claim?*), and because it starts with the line: "Have you banished the love that you had for me?" (ibid., 4:324–25). Thetis was then substituted for Cyrene because Thetis is a destructive mother. She meant to help her son Achilles, but she failed to protect him adequately. When she dipped her infant child in the waters of the Styx to make him immortal, she left him vulnerable at the heel where she was holding him, and that is where Achilles was eventually to receive a mortal wound. She failed him. One more reason for fusing Achilles and Aristaeus may have been that Aristaeus pursued Eurydice, Orpheus's wife, to rape her (this too is in Vergil), causing her to step on a snake that bit her heel, and thus to die. The choice of the heel further suggests, via fetishism, that the wound suffered because of the mother's dereliction and thus inflicted by the mother is a screen for castration. If so, then the power of the mythological given is that it unites two symbolisms of rejection: maternal rejection and social rejection (and, furthermore, the society ladies who will finally accept the narrator are clearly maternal figures).

When Proust alludes to the myth, it is, revealingly, to say that Vergil shows Aristaeus received in the watery underworld *à bras ouverts* ("with open arms").[22] Vergil does not say that (in fact, Aristaeus is at first kept out), but the phrase is a commonplace metaphor both for social acceptance and for a mother's embrace. The allusion to Aristaeus is, moreover, as farfetched as can be, totally unmotivated within the narrative (but perhaps differently motivated, since it awkwardly exemplifies a case of reverse snobbery). It can therefore only be truth unwittingly surfacing from the depths. But all this is irrelevant to readers, for it plays no role in their grasping the import and the symbolism of the aquarium wall subtext.

What does play a role in helping them to uncover the hidden truth is the presence of ungrammaticalities in the mimesis, of unacceptable images—in short, of faults or rents in the fabric of verisimilitude.

In order for these ungrammaticalities to be properly understood and to work as clues to the interpretation of symbolic subtexts, they must affect the predication that carries the symbolism. Alone, outside of such a sign system, ungrammaticalities only point to the psychological unconscious and cannot guide anyone but an analyst. There is, for instance, a daydreaming sequence early in the novel in which the narrator expresses his attraction to the Guermantes way, to the Guermantes name, and his sexual fixation on the Duchesse de Guermantes herself, as yet personally unknown to him. He does so by rationalizing: the country around the Guermantes *château* is pleasant to him because it is full of picturesque rivers. He even has a dream in which he is a guest of the duchess's and she teaches him the art of trout fishing. This is crazy enough, but the telling detail is the use of that rarest of adjectives, *fluviatile*, to speak of a countryside that is simply full of streams, and specifically not of large rivers, to which *fluviatile*, or more commonly, *fluvial*, generally refers. The next time Proust uses *fluviatile*, it is, unaccountably, to speak of places "*fluviatile* and poetic"[23]:

> [I] seemed to have before my eyes a fragment of that fluvial country which I had longed much to see and know since coming upon a description of it by one of my favourite authors. And it was with that story-book land, with its imagined soil intersected by a hundred bubbling watercourses, that Guermantes, changing its aspect in my mind, became identfed.[24]

"One of my favourite authors" is, in fact, Vergil himself. *Fluviatile*, a hyperlatinate form, echoes and concentrates the whole impact of Aristaeus's awe when, admitted to his mother's realm, he sees "all the big rivers flowing under the vast earth."[25] The whole passage is a tremendous mimetic feat on Vergil's part, as he tries to cope with a description that has to transform a normal landscape into an imaginary netherworld—so much for proving that the duchess is a mother image. To cap all this, there is a line, "the sad Aristaeus stands in tears near the waters of the river Peneus, the fatherly one" (ibid., 4:355), *Penei genitoris ad undam*, where the name of the River Peneus in the genitive case, *Penei genitoris*, is nearly identical with the Latin for generating penis (*penis genitoris*).

I have dwelt at length on this example because of *fluviatile* more than anything else: the rare form chosen by Proust is evidently like a signal that the Latin source is returning to the surface of the text, like a sign that stands for the whole intertext. If the written text functions like a screen (in the psychoanalytical sense of the word), it is to be expected that it will also, as in our dreams, contain an index pointing to where the anamnesis begins.

While these watery allusions unite the themes of social and sexual desire, the principal representation of desire in Proust's opus is the *passe/passer/passé* subtext that recurs throughout most of the novel. This mimesis of libido centers on the theme of prostitution practiced by or inflicted upon the love object. The theme's explicit form is the motif of the house of assignation: the *maison de passe*, where the narrator imagines the desired woman, or where he thinks of finding a willing and exciting partner, or where he fantasizes his loved one having a fling with someone else. Needless to say, we have more here than just an effective fantasy of maximum availability of the sex object coupled with juicy desecration: in terms both of narrative suspense and of a diegesis that emphasizes social barriers, thus multiplying the hurdles that fan the flames of desire, the *maison de passe* is *the* solution for the seeker of pleasure and the most pregnant valorization of the first component meaning of the *passe* syllepsis:

> It was about this time that Bloch overthrew my conception of the world and opened for me fresh possibilities of happiness (which . . . were to change later on into possibilities of suffering), by assuring me that, contrary to all that I had believed at the time of my walks along the Méséglise way, women never asked for anything better than to make love. He added to this service a second . . . it was he who took me for the first time into a house of assignation. He had indeed told me that there were any number of pretty women whom one might enjoy.[26]

Whereas this theme determines a number of recurrences of our key word, the second meaning of the word, or rather, in this case, its homonym, is still needed for the syllepsis to catch fire, and for the theme to become but one of the components of the *passe* subtext. This homonym or quasi-homonym is supplied by *passante*, "passerby," and *passer*, "to pass," including the whole gamut of acceptations this verb has, from walking by to the passing of all that is ephemeral.

The one love story that organizes the whole *Recherche* seems to be built in order to actualize, focus upon, and valorize *passer/passante*. It begins with the narrator's accession to sexual awareness and ends with this accession to a proper interpretation of time. The story caps the whole edifice in *Le Temps retrouvé* with a social triumph that signals the complete reversal of the system of class or group exclusion on which every subplot hinges. This is, of course, the story of Gilberte Swann, from her first steps as an upstart, the daughter of a Jew and of a demimondaine, to her ultimate success as the adoptive daughter of one paragon of the French nobility and the wife of another. The tale of the narrator's desire for her gradually meshes into the quest for a certain Mlle. de l'Orgeville who, he has been told, slakes her sensual

FICTIONAL TRUTH

thirst in the place where Marcel has dreamt of taking her in his turn. It is significant that Gilberte's husband, Saint-Loup, should have been the one who gave Mlle. de l'Orgeville's name to the narrator and that Gilberte should strive to imitate Rachel, Saint-Loup's former mistress, who is also a frequenter of bawdyhouses. The phrase *maison de passe*, directly or indirectly, penetrates the image of Gilberte, until we reach the point where the diegetic time and place of both women become one, when the narrator makes eye contact with a young lady on the street and convinces himself that she is his long-sought prey, only to discover that she is none other than Gilberte, whom he has not seen for years (ibid., 3:562ff.; 3:573ff.). The crossing or fusion of diegetic sequences is confirmed by the narrator's confusion of the bad girl's name with that of Gilberte's adoptive father. Gilberte is perfectly conscious that Marcel had pursued her as he would a whore (ibid., 3:573–74; 3:586–87). This interweaving of two narratives finally climaxes in *Le Temps retrouvé*, with Gilberte's reminiscing about her childhood: the separate subtexts become one retrospectively with the mimesis of the past in Gilberte's recollection now mirroring the narrators.

She reminds him of the equivocal gesture that she made as a little girl, one that at the time only puzzled the little boy that he was, but a gesture that would have been quite unequivocal coming from a woman:

> "How I loved you then!"
> She replied: "Why didn't you tell me? I loved you too. In fact I flung myself twice at your head . . . I signalled to you so vulgarly that I am ashamed of it to this day . . . And the second time was when I passed you on the street . . . I did not recognize you at first, or rather I did unconsciously recognize you because I felt the same attraction as I had felt at Tansonville."[27]

The equation could not be made clearer between her behavior in the most distant past and her behavior later when she felt aroused by an unknown passerby and wished he had treated her as a slut. Readers cannot avoid responding to this most powerful of commonplaces, which, despite appearances, is less a common Gallic street experience than a fantasy consecrated in familiar sterotypes: the desire for a beautiful woman met by chance on the street with whom a gaze is exchanged, never to be seen again, and leaving behind the bitter regret of a love, of a life that might have been. Of the several nineteenth-century versions of the theme, the best-known is Baudelaire's "A une Passante" ("To a Woman Passing By"), the intertext in Proust's passage:

The deafening street howled around me.
Tall, slim, in deep mourning, majestic grief,
A woman passed, elaborately raising
And swinging her openwork hem;

Graceful and noble, the legs of a statue.
As for me, I was drinking, tense as a madman,
In her eye, livid sky where the storm brews,
The softness that fascinates, the pleasure that kills.

A flash—then night! Fugitive beauty
Whose glance has caused my sudden rebirth,
Will I never see you again before eternity?

Elsewhere, far from here! Too late—maybe never.
For I can't see where you've fled, you don't know where I'm
    going,
O you I might have loved, you who knew it well.[28]

It is easy to see that this intertext loads *passante* with the same libidinal symbolism as *maison de passe*, and that the two words are now ready for mutual substitutability or for the sylleptic interface.

Substitutability: the fortuitous encounter with a *passante* begets a vast subtext dispersed throughout the novel, which consistently displaces *passante*, the most natural word, in favor of the verb *passer*, and which therefore functions as a periphrasis for the noun. Revealingly, *passser* appears in a person, tense, and mood that make it identical with *passe*. It is as though that coarse synonym for random sex, superimposed on *passante*, had privileged its root at the expense of the *-ante* ending, toying with a pseudo-etymology that makes a *passante* a woman who frequents houses of ill repute. As further proof of the power of this combination, the verb saturates the subtext, against all literary rules of elegant variation. Moreover, in the following variant to the subtext, the replacement of plain *passante* by what she is good at generates a deliriously improbable translation of the street encounter into the encounter of clouds on a windy day, in which iterative *passe* alone suffices to sexualize the sky itself.

> Her eyes . . . gave the impression of nobility, as on days of high wind the air, though invisible, lets us perceive the speed with which it is passing (*il passe*) between us and the sky. For a moment her eyes met mine, like those travelling skies on stormy days which approach a slower cloud, touch it, pass it by (*la dépassent*). But they do not know one another, and are soon driven far apart. So, now, our looks were for a moment confronted, each ignorant of what the celestial continent that lay before it held by way of promises or threats for the future. Only at the moment when her gaze passed precisely under mine (*passa exactement sous le mien*) without slackening its pace it clouded over slightly. So on a clear night the wind-swept moon passes (*passe*) behind a cloud, veils its brightness for a moment, but soon reappears.[29]

Sylleptic interface: the most telling example is also the last episode of *Le Temps retrouvé*. It is fitting that the scene, a

party at the Guermantes's at which the narrator meets people he used to know, now metamorphosed by old age, would
be the most complete version of the *passe* subtext. In this
scene, the *passe* antanaclasis, having exhaused all possible variations of the sylleptic given, finally annexes *passé*, "the past,"
the key word of *Temps retrouvé*, in the same way that *passe*
had embedded itself in *passante*. Among the guests, the narrator meets an aristocratic lady who used to pick up sexual
partners on the street, another familiar fantasy (with the
spice of polarity: the haughty noblewoman can be had). Intertextually, she is a variant on the Duchesse de Guermantes he
had so desired years before, whom *he* would pass every morn-
ing and whose conquest is now realized through a stand-in:

> Born almost on the steps of a throne, three times married, richly
> kept for years at a time by great bankers, not to mention the
> countless whims in which she had permitted herself to indulge,
> she bore lightly beneath her gown, mauve like her wonderful
> round eyes and her painted face, the slightly tangled memories
> of the innumerable affairs of her life. As she passed near me, mak-
> ing her discreet exit, I bowed to her. She recognized me, took my
> hand and pressed it, and fixed upon me the round mauve pupils
> which seemed to say: "How long it is since we have seen each
> other! We must talk about all that another time." Her pressure
> on my hand became a squeeze, for she had a vague idea that one
> evening in her carriage, when she had offered to drop me at my
> door after a party at the Duchesse de Guermantes's, there might
> have been an encounter between us. Just to be on the safe side,
> she seemed to allude to something that had in fact never hap-
> pened ... She merely looked at me in the manner which sig-
> nified: "How long it is!" and in which one caught a momentary
> glimpse of her husbands and the men who had kept her and two
> wars, while her stellar eyes, like an astronomical clock cut in a
> block of opal, marked successively all those solemn hours of a
> distant past which she rediscovered every time she wanted to bid
> you a casual good-bye.[30]

The accumulation of homonyms of *passe* carries readers irresistibly forward: *les souvenirs . . . de ce passé innombrable* ("the memories of her rich past"). *Comme elle passait devant moi* ("as she passed before me"), *une passade entre nous* ("an affair between us," literally, a "fling"), the years *où repassaient . . . les hommes qui l'avaient entretenue . . . les heures solennelles du passé* ("the years in which the men who had kept her passed again, the solemn hours of the past").

The cumulative effect is obsessive and, indeed, awkward, which is, as I have pointed out, unavoidable, since it is insistently motivated by the syllepsis and the other words engendered by several referents. More importantly, as the *passe* derivation now overtakes *passé* (the one paronym that syllepsis had not yet absorbed), the accelerating momentum magnifies the word into a periphrastic grand finale, the crazy image of the *passante* metamorphosed into an astronomical clock. This is no mere coincidence between *passé* as the synonym of *temps retrouvé* and *passé* as the last contextually feasible variant of *passe*. The subtext's clausula does not merely coincide with the novel's dénouement: it translates it into the code of desire. It cannot be by chance that the eyes of the *passante* tell the time instead of the hands of a regular clock: it is because eye contact is the medium of desire for the *passante* and the imminence of her availability. The *passante* has returned for the consummation of pleasure, canceling out the tantalizing barrier of desire, replacing it with fulfillment and doing so disguised in the garb of time, because *temps retrouvé* is the resolution of the narrator's anxiety and its re-presentation is the passing arrested.

Antanaclasis soon makes it impossible for the reader to understand any single alternate meaning of the original syllepsis without repressing the others, suppressing them in the text and making them very present to his mind as a result. This latent presence or denial of pertinence functions exactly like the unconscious/conscious pair in the psyche.

As a result of this tension or polarization that makes the said and the unsaid work together against all logic and at the expense of mimetic referentiality, readers find themselves compelled to perform a hermeneutic procedure not unlike analysis but whose first effect is that they have a sense of unlocking, of uncovering. This is equivalent to a pattern of truth, whether or not consistent with actual truth, and with or without truth content; on this model readers are made to perform an exercise in truth finding.

This callisthenics combines in narrative with two other factors: the tautological derivations described in the first chapter and the saturation observed in subtexts of the paradigmatic type. A repetitive mechanical sequence of symbols and syllepsis thus demands of readers a performative reading, a ritual equivalent of the experience of truth in real life.

Finally, antanaclasis as a special kind of subtext, one born of a syllepsis, is the agency through which the narrative accedes to fiction, and fiction, to truth. It replaces uncertain or even undecidable readings of the narrative sequence of causes and effects and subjective perceptions of the diegesis with the evidence of simultaneous formal equivalencies. In this respect, however, antanaclasis only displays more visibly a mechanism common to all subtexts. Because of the subtext's mnemonic function, any reference, however fragmentary it may be, to that subtext tells its whole story and activates its full symbolism. Any such reference is like a meta-linguistic insert within the narrative. As a result, the reader, deciphering it and rebuilding the whole from the part actualized at any particular point, already knows the end of the story or the aims of the characters. The subtext has no future nor does it have a past, since the whole development is referred to at once either intratextually by reverting to the subtext's generator, to the sememe of the word that produced it in the first place, or intertextually, in the case of the unconscious framework that is syllepsis. What is left of the story is a state of affairs, an end product, the explanation for that state of affairs and the exemplarity of both. The subtext is thus, as an embedding, a hermeneutic model translating any narrative action, situation, or event that fits that model into its own interpretive discourse. Representation within the model is no longer time oriented but given as a whole, as a symbol, as a summation of all the initial sememe's potential consequences that may develop. Thus unchanging and complete, it is an image of truth.

Paradoxically, therefore, fictional truth results from two eliminations: first, the suppression or suspension of verisimilitude; and second, the elimination or suspension of the component of time or duration in the narrative. Fictional truth obtains when the mode of the diegesis shifts from the narrative to the poetic. This is the ultimate avatar of the referential illusion that replaces in literature the reference to reality with a reference to language. Since we are now dealing with a different kind of truth, so also is a different kind of referential illusion needed to found it. Archimedes claimed that his lever would lift the entire world if only he could find a fulcrum outside that world. Similarly, symbolic truth needs a reference outside the narrative. Nothing is more essential to the narrative than temporality; therefore, its truth must transcend time. By coincidence, the lack of vulnerability to time is also part of our commonplace ideas about truth. Subtexts, therefore, and the intertextuality that sets them in motion, do not unfold along an axis of duration. Like the unconscious described by Freud, the unconscious of fiction and, therefore, its truth, stands outside the realm of time and is impervious to its ravages.

Notes

CHAPTER 1   TRUTH IN DIEGESIS

1. Gérard Genette, *Figures II* (Paris: Seuil, 1969), 98–99.

2. Marcel Proust, *Contre Sainte-Beuve* (Paris: Gallimard, 1954), 120: "Il n'y avait encore personne devant l'église, sauf la dame en noir qu'on en voit sortir rapidement à toute heure dans les villes de province" (my translation).

3. Henry James, *Washington Square* (New York: Penguin, 1981), chap. 24, 121.

4. Jane Austen, *Pride and Prejudice,* ed. Donald J. Gray (New York: W. W. Norton, 1966), vol. 3, chap. 1, 166–67.

5. Anthony Trollope, *The Duke's Children* (Oxford: Oxford Univ. Press, 1977), chap. 38, 304.

6. Lewis Carroll, "The Hunting of the Snark," in *Complete Works* (New York: The Modern Library, 1950), 757.

7. George Meredith, *The Egoist* (New York: Penguin, 1979), chap. 5, 78.

1. George Eliot, *Middlemarch* (New York: Penguin, 1965), chap. 20, 230.

2. Trollope, *Barchester Towers* (Oxford: Oxford Univ. Press, 1953), vol. 2, chap. 30, 32.

3. Meir Sternberg, "Mimesis and Motivation: The Two Faces of Fictional Coherence," in *Literary Criticism and Philosophy, Yearbook of Comparative Criticism* (University Park: Pennsylvania State Univ. Press, 1983), 10:153.

4. Honoré de Balzac, *Illusions Perdues*, ed. Marcel Bouteron (Paris: Gallimard, 1952), 4:467: "Jérôme-Nicolas Séchard, fidèle à la destinée que son nom lui avait faite, était doué d'une soif inextinguible."

5. Balzac, *Z. Marcas*, 7:736: "Entre les faits de la vie et le nom des hommes, il est de secrètes et d'inexplicables concordances ou des désaccords visibles qui surprennent ... Peut-être reviendra-t-on quelque jour aux Sciences occultes.

Ne voyez-vous pas dans la construction du Z une allure contrariée? Ne figure-t-elle pas le zigzag aléatoire et fantasque d'une vie tourmentée?"

6. Trollope, *The Three Clerks* (Oxford: Oxford Univ. Press, 1925), chap. 35, 480–83.

7. Proust, *A la Recherche du temps perdu*, ed. Pierre Clarac and André Ferré (Paris: Gallimard, 1954), 2:854–55: "Nous étions, Albertine et moi, devant la station Balbec du petit train d'intérêt local. Nous nous étions fait conduire par l'omnibus de l'hôtel, à cause du mauvais temps. Non loin de nous était M. Nissim Bernard, lequel avait un oeil poché. Il trompait depuis peu l'enfant des choeurs d'*Athalie* avec le garçon d'une ferme assez achalandée du voisinage, 'Aux Cerisiers.' Ce garçon rouge, aux traits abrupts, avait absolument l'air d'avoir comme tête une tomate. Une tomate exactement semblable servait de tête à son frère jumeau. Pour le contemplateur désintéressé, il y a à cela d'assez beau, dans ces ressemblances parfaites de deux jumeaux, que la nature, comme si elle s'était momentanément industrialisée, semble débiter des produit pareils. Malheureusement, le point de vue de M. Nissim Bernard était autre et cette ressemblance n'était qu'extérieure. La

tomate no. 2 se plaisait avec frénésie à faire exclusivement les délices des dames, la tomate no. 1 ne détestait pas condescendre aux goûts de certains messieurs. Or chaque fois que, secoué, ansi que par un réflexe, par le souvenir des bonnes heures passées avec la tomate no. 1, M. Bernard se présentait 'Aux Cerisiers,' myope (et du reste la myopie n'était pas nécessaire pour les confondre), le vieil Israélite, jouant sans le savoir Amphitryon, s'adressait au frère jumeau et lui disait: "Veux-tu me donner rendez-vous pour ce soir?" Il recevait aussitôt une solide 'tournée.' Elle vint même à se renouveler au cours d'un même repas, où il continuait avec l'autre les propos commencés avec le premier."

I have used the C. K. Scott Moncrieff and Terence Kilmartin translation, *Remembrance of Things Past* (New York: Random House, 1981) with slight modifications where appropriate. Volume and page references are to the Pléiade edition and the translation, respectively.

8. Ibid., 2:855; 2:884: "A la longue elle le dégoûta tellement, par association d'idées, des tomates, même de celles comestibles, que chaque fois qu'il entendait un voyageur en commander à côté de lui, au Grand-Hôtel, il lui chuchotait: 'Excusez-moi, Monsieur, de m'adresser à vous, sans vous connaître. Mais j'ai entendu que vous commandiez des tomates. Elles sont pourries aujourd'hui. Je vous le dis dans votre intérêt car pour moi cela m'est égal, je n'en prends jamais.' L'étranger remerciait avec effusion ce voisin philanthrope et désintéressé, rappelait le garçon, feignait de se raviser: 'Non, décidément, pas de tomates.' Aimé, qui connaissait la scène, en riait tour seul et pensait: 'C'est un vieux malin que Monsieur Bernard, il a encore trouvé le moyen de faire changer la commande.'"

9. Charles Dickens, *Little Dorrit,* ed. R. D. McMaster (New York: Odyssey Press, 1969), bk. 1, chap. 21, 230.

10. *Illusions Perdues,* 4:470: "Là était l'évier sur lequel se lavaient avant et après le tirage les Formes, ou pour employer le langage vulgaire, les planches de caractères; il s'en échappait une décoction d'encre mêlée aux eaux ménagères de la maison, qui faisait croire aux paysans venus les jour de marché que le diable se débarbouillait dans cette maison."

11. Ibid., 4:468: "Sa femme avait pendant longtemps contenu dans de justes bornes cette passion pour le raisin pilé, goût si naturel aux Ours que M. de Chateaubriand l'a remarqué chez les véritables ours de

l'Amerique; mais les philosophes ont observé que les habitudes du jeune âge reviennent avec force dans la vieillesse de l'homme. Séchard confirmait cette loi morale: plus il vieillissait, plus il aimait à boire."

12. *A la Recherche du temps perdu*, 2:575; 2:597–98: "Il se montra peu aimable. Aussi, bien que descendues des hauteurs de l'hôtel de Bréquigny pour voir la duchesse (ou plutôt pour lui annoncer le caractère alarmant, et incompatible pour les parents avec les réunions mondaines, de la maladie de leur cousin), ne restèrent-elles pas longtemps, et, munies de leur bâton d'alpiniste, Walpurge et Dorothée (tels étaient les prénoms des deux soeurs) reprirent la route escarpée de leur faîte."

13. Ibid., 2:572–73; 2:594–95: "Jusqu'à cet hôtel (qui était celui de leur père, M. de Bréquigny), rien que des corps de bâtiments peu élevés, orientés des façons les plus diverses et qui, sans arrêter la vue, prolongeaient la distance, de leurs plans obliques. La tourelle en tuiles rouges de la remise où le marquis de Frécourt garait ses voitures, se terminait bien par une aiguille plus haute, mais si mince qu'elle ne cachait rien, et faisait penser à ces jolies constructions anciennes de la Suisse qui s'élancent, isolées, au pied d'une montagne. Tous ces points vagues et divergents où se reposaient les yeux, faisaient paraître plus éloigné que s'il avait été séparé de nous par plusieurs rues ou de nombreux contreforts l'hôtel de Mme de Plassac, en réalité assez voisin mais chimériquement éloigné comme un paysage alpestre."

14. Ibid., 2:573; 2:595: "On avait, à suivre aux différents étages les valets de pied impossibles à bien distinguer, mais qui battaient des tapis, le même plaisir qu'à voir, dans un paysage de Turner ou d'Elstir, un voyageur en diligence, ou un guide, à différents degrés d'altitude du Saint-Gothard."

15. Ibid., 2:725; 2:751: "Il se heurta devant sa porte, sévèrement gardée par elles, aux deux dames à canne qui n'avaient pas craint de descendre nuitamment de leur cime afin d'empêcher un scandale. 'Basin, nous avons tenu à vous prévenir, de peur que vous ne soyez vu à cette redoute: le pauvre Amanien vient de mourir, il y a une heure.' Le duc eut un instant d'alarme. Il voyait la fameuse redoute s'effondrer pour lui du moment que, par ces maudites montagnardes, il était averti de la mort de M. d'Osmond. Mais il se ressaisit bien vite et lança aux deux cousines ce mot où il faisait entrer, avec la détermination de ne pas renoncer

à un plaisir, son incapacité d'assimiler exactement les tours de la langue française: 'Il est mort! Mais non, on exagère, on exagère!'"

CHAPTER 3   SYMBOLIC SYSTEMS IN NARRATIVE

1. See M. Riffaterre, "The Making of the Text," in *Identity of the Literary Text*, ed. Mario J. Valdés and Owen Miller (Toronto: Univ. of Toronto Press, 1985), esp. 61–63.

2. E. M. Forster, *A Passage to India* (New York: Harcourt, Brace, Jovanovich, 1984), chap. 7, 64–65.

3. *Contre Sainte-Beuve*, ed. Bernard de Fallois (Paris: Gallimard, 1954), 220–21.

4. Balzac, *Le Curé de Tours*, ed. Marcel Bouteron (Paris: Bibliothèque de la Pléiade, 1952), 3:838: "Telle était la substance des phrases jetées en avant par les tuyaux capillaires du grand conciliabule femelle, et complaisamment répétées par la ville de Tours."

5. Ibid., 829: "Ces personnes, logées toutes dans la ville de manière à y figurer les vaisseaux capillaires d'une plante, aspiraient, avec la soif d'une feuille pour la rosée, les nouvelles, les secrets de chaque ménage, les pompaient et les transmettaient machinalement à l'abbé Troubert, comme les feuilles communiquent à la tige la fraîcheur qu'elles ont absorbée."

6. Trollope, *He Knew He Was Right* (Oxford: Oxford Univ. Press, 1978), chap. 15, 141.

7. James, *The Golden Bowl*, (New York: Penguin, 1981), chap. 6, 108–9.

8. Ibid., 119–20. Emphases are mine, except for *had* and *then*.

9. Ibid., 120. The next two quotations appear on 121.

10. We are told (chap. 4, 80–82) that the connection between the prince's Italian namesake and Maggie's homeland of which he was "namefather" (81) became romantic for Maggie. The eyewitness says to herself: "By that sign . . . he'll conquer . . . It really *was*, practically, the fine side of the wedge" (81), a nice, if unconscious, way to repeat the oxymoron of negative angularity (*wedge*) with positive use (*fine side, conquer*). Even when the flawed bowl finally breaks, it keeps together the seemingly incompatible angularity (423: "the split was so sharp") and

smoothness (424: "the bowl might still quite beautifully . . . have passed for uninjured").

11. *A la Recherche du temps perdu*, 1:418; 1:453: "Pensant que le Beau — dans l'ordre des élégances féminines — était régi par des lois occultes à la connaissance desquelles elles avaient été initiées, et qu'elle avaient le pouvoir de le réaliser, j'acceptais d'avance comme une révélation l'apparition de leur toilette, de leur attelage, de mille détails au sein desquels je mettais ma croyance comme une âme intérieure qui donnait la cohésion d'un chef-d'oeuvre à cet ensemble éphémère et mouvant. Mais c'est Mme Swann que je voulais voir."

12. Ibid., 1:417–18; 1:452: "[Le Bois] était pour moi comme ces jardins zoologiques où l'on voit rassemblés des flores diverses et des paysages opposés, où après une colline on trouve une grotte, un pré, des rochers, une rivière, une fosse, une colline, un marais, mais où l'on sait qu'ils ne sont là que pour fournir aux ébats de l'hippopotame, des zèbres, des crocodiles, des lapins russes, des ours et du héron, un milieu approprié ou un cadre pittoresque; lui, le Bois, complexe aussi, réunissant des petits mondes divers et clos — faisant succéder quelque ferme plantée d'arbres rouges, de chênes d'Amérique, comme une exploitation agricole dans la Virginie, à une sapinière au bord du lac, ou à une futaie d'où surgit tout à coup dans sa souple fourrure, avec les beaux yeux d'une bête, quelque promeneuse rapide —, il était le Jardin des femmes; et — comme l'allée de Myrtes de l'*Enéide* —, plantée pour elles d'arbres d'une seule essence, l'allée des Acacias était fréquentée par les Beautés célèbres."

13. Ibid., 2:285; 2:295: " . . . Les jardins, ne sont que des Ersatz, des succédanés, des alibis. Dans le fond de notre tonneau, comme Diogène, nous demandons un homme. Nous cultivons les bégonias, nous taillons les ifs, par pis aller, parce que les ifs et les bégonias se laissent faire. Mais nous aimerions mieux donner notre temps à un arbuste humain."

14. Ibid., 1:418 and 421; 1:452: "Comme l'allée de Myrtes de l'*Enéide* — plantée pour elles d'arbres d'une seule essence, l'allée des Acacias était fréquentée par les Beautés célèbres . . . l'allée de la Reine-Marguerite où vont les femmes qui cherchent à être seules, ou à avoir l'air de chercher à l'être."

15. Ibid., 1:418; 1:452: "le faîte aperçu de leur frondaison légère et

mièvre, d'une élégance facile, d'une coupe coquette et d'un mince tissu [. .] enfin jusqu'à leur nom féminin, désoeuvré et doux, me faisaient battre le coeur."

16. Ibid., 1:424; 1:459: "Forcés depuis tant d'années par une sorte de greffe à vivre en commun avec la femme, [les arbres] m'évoquaient la dryade, la belle mondaine rapide et colorée qu'au passage ils couvrent de leurs branches et obligent à ressentir comme eux la puissance de la saison."

17. Ibid., 1:424–25; 1:459: "Ces chevaux furieux et légers comme des guêpes, les yeux injectés de sang comme les cruels chevaux de Diomède, et que maintenant, pris d'un désir de revoir ce que j'avais aimé, aussi ardent que celui qui me poussait bien des années auparavant dans ces mêmes chemins, je voulais avoir de nouveau sous les yeux, au moment où l'énorme cocher de Mme Swann, surveillé par un petit groom gros comme le poing et aussi enfantin que saint Georges, essayait de maîtriser leurs ailes d'acier qui se débattaient effarouchées et palpitantes."

18. Ibid., 1:419; 1:453: "emportée par le vol de deux chevaux ardents, minces et contournés comme on en voit dans les dessins de Constantin Guys."

19. Ibid., 1:427; 1:462: "Le soleil s'était caché. La nature recommençait à régner sur le Bois d'où s'était envolée l'idée qu'il était le Jardin élyséen de la Femme; au-dessus du moulin factice le vrai ciel était gris; le vent ridait le Grand Lac de petites vaguelettes, comme un lac; de gros oiseaux parcouraient rapidement le Bois, comme un bois."

CHAPTER 4   THE UNCONSCIOUS OF FICTION

1. Victor Hugo, *L'Homme qui rit* (1869), bk. 7, chap.3, 424 (Paris: Ollendorff, 1907): "Ses mauvaises pensées devenues chair vivante."

2. Ibid., 422: "Elle dormait la tête renversée, un de ses pieds refoulant ses couvertures, comme la succube au-dessus de laquelle le rêve bat des ailes."

3. Ibid.: " . . . une chose formidable, une femme nue."

4. Ibid.: "Entre sa nudité et le regard il y avait deux obstacles, sa chemise, et le rideau de gaze d'argent, deux transparences."

5. Ibid., 423: "Etait-ce une fille? Etait-ce une vierge? Les deux. Messaline, présente peut-être dans l'invisible, devait sourire, et Diane devait veiller. Il y avait sur cette beauté la clarté de l'inaccessible."

6. Ibid., 421: "Bain noir fait pour changer la blancheur en resplendissement."

7. Ibid., 425: "Par instants la duchesse se déplaçait mollement sur le lit, et avait les vagues mouvements d'une vapeur dans l'azur, changeant d'attitude comme la nuée change de forme."

8. Ibid., p. 431: "Tu arrives, voilà mon âme dehors. Je ne la connaissais pas. Elle est surprenante. Ton approche fait sortir l'hydre de moi, déesse. Tu me révèles ma vraie nature."

9. Hugo, *Les Travailleurs de la mer* (1866) pt. 2, bk. 1, chap. 13 (Paris: Garnier-Flammarion, 1980), 405: "une femme toute nue . . . était probablement sur cet autel tout à l'heure."

10. *L'Homme qui rit*, 432: "'Le difforme est l'envers du sublime.'"

11. *Les Travailleurs de la mer*, pt. 2, bk. 1, chap. 11, 397: "une caverne extraordinaire."

12. *L'Homme qui rit*, 420.

13. *Les Misérables* (1862), ed. Maurice Allem (Paris: Bibliothèque de la Pléiade, 1951), 743: "Ce fut un étrange éclair. Elle baissa les yeux, et il continua son chemin. Ce qu'il venait de voir, ce n'était pas l'oeil ingénu et simple d'une enfant, c'était un gouffre mystérieux qui s'était entr'ouvert, puis brusquement refermé. Il y a un jour où toute jeune fille regarde ainsi. Malheur à qui se trouve là!"

14. Ibid., 744: "Toutes les puretés et toutes les ardeurs se concentrent dans ce rayon céleste et fatal qui, plus que les oeillades les mieux travaillées des coquettes, a le pouvoir magique de faire subitement éclore au fond d'une âme cette fleur sombre, pleine de parfums et de poisons, qu'on appelle l'amour."

15. Ibid., 750: "Le regard des femmes ressemble à de certains rouages tranquilles en apparence et formidables. On passe à côté tous les jours paisiblement et impunément et sans se douter de rien. Il vient un moment où l'on oublie même que cette chose est là. On va, on vient, on rêve, on parle, on rit. Tout à coup on se sent saisi. C'est fini. Le rouage vous tient, le regard vous a pris. Il vous a pris, n'importe par où ni comment, par une partie quelconque de votre pensée qui traînait, par une

distraction que vous avez eue. Vous êtes perdu. Vous y passerez tout entier. Un enchaînement de forces mystérieuses s'empare de vous. Vous vous débattez en vain. Plus de secours humain possible. Vous allez tomber d'engrenage en engrenage, d'angoisse en angoisse, de torture en torture, vous, votre esprit, votre fortune, votre avenir, votre âme; et, selon que vous serez au pouvoir d'une créature méchante ou d'un noble coeur, vous ne sortirez de cette effrayante machine que défiguré par la honte ou transfiguré par la passion."

16. *Les Travailleurs de la mer*, 498: "Méduse servie par huit serpents."

17. Ibid., 498: " . . . englué, impuissant, vous vous sentez lentement vidé dans cet épouvantable sac, qui est un monstre."

18. Ibid.: "La ventouse, c'est vous-même qui entrez dans la bête."

19. *A la Recherche du temps perdu*, 2:40; 2:36: "Après commençaient les fauteuils d'orchestre, le séjour des mortels à jamais séparé du sombre et transparent royaume auquel çà et là servaient de frontière, dans leur surface liquide et plane, les yeux limpides et réfléchissants des déesses des eaux. Car les strapontins du rivage, les formes des monstres de l'orchestre se peignaient dans ces yeux suivant les seules lois de l'optique et selon leur angle d'incidence, comme il arrive pour ces deux parties de la réalité extérieure auxquelles, sachant qu'elles ne possèdent pas, si rudimentaire soit-elle, d'âme analogue à la nôtre, nous nous jugerions insensés d'adresser un sourire ou un regard: les minéraux et les personnes avec qui nous ne sommes pas en relations."

20. Ibid., 1:682; 1:733: "tandis que les amis du jeune homme riche l'enviaient d'avoir une maîtresse si bien habillée, les écharpes de celle-ci tendaient devant la petite société comme un voile parfumé et souple, mais qui la séparait du monde."

21. Vergil, *Georgics*, 4.363.

22. *A la recherche du temps perdu*, 1:18; 1:19.

23. Ibid., 1:389; 1:422 (this phrase occurs in a later context).

24. Ibid., 1:172; 1:188: "il me semblait avoir sous les yeux un fragment de cette région fluviatile que je désirais tant connaître depuis que je l'avais vue décrite par un de mes écrivains préférés. Et ce fut avec elle, avec son sol imaginaire traversé de cours d'eau bouillonnants, que Guermantes, changeant d'aspect dans ma pensée, s'identifia."

25. *Georgics*, 4.366.

26. *A la recherche du temps perdu,* 1:575–76; 1:619: "Ce fut vers cette époque que Bloch bouleversa ma conception du monde, ouvrit pour moi des possibilités nouvelles de bonheur (qui devaient du reste se changer plus tard en possibilités de souffrance), en m'assurant que, contrairement à ce que je croyais au temps de mes promenades du côté de Méséglise, les femmes ne demandaient jamais mieux que de faire l'amour. Il compléta ce service en m'en rendant un second que je ne devais apprécier que beaucoup plus tard: ce fut lui qui me conduisit pour la première fois dans une maison de passe. Il m'avait bien dit qu'il y avait beaucoup de jolies femmes qu'on peut posséder."

27. Ibid., 3:693–94; 3:711–12: "'Comme je vous aimais alors!' Elle me répondit: 'Pourquoi ne me le disiez-vous pas? je ne m'en étais pas doutée. Moi je vous aimais. Et même deux fois je me suis jetée à votre tête . . . je vous l'ai indiqué d'une façon tellement crue que j'en ai honte maintenant'. . . 'Et la seconde fois, reprit Gilberte, c'est, bien des années après, quand je vous ai rencontré sous votre porte, la veille du jour où je vous ai retrouvé chez ma tante Oriane; je ne vous ai pas reconnu tout de suite, ou plutôt je vous reconnaissais sans le savoir puisque j'avais la même envie qu'à Tansonville.'"

28. Charles Baudelaire *Oeuvres complètes,* ed. Claude Pichois (Paris: Gallimard, 1975), 1:92, trans. Elisabeth Ladenson.

A une Passante

La rue assourdissante autour de moi hurlait.
Longue, mince, en grand deuil, douleur majestueuse,
Une femme passa, d'une main fastueuse
Soulevant, balançant le feston et l'ourlet;

Agile et noble, avec sa jambe de statue.
Moi, je buvais, crispé comme un extravagant,
Dans son oeil, ciel livide où germe l'ouragan,
La douceur qui fascine et le plaisir qui tue.

Un éclair . . . puis la nuit! —Fugitive beauté
Dont le regard m'a fait soudainement renaître,
Ne te verrai-je plus que dans l'éternité?

Ailleurs, bien loin d'ici! trop tard! *jamais* peut-être!
Car j'ignore où tu fuis, tu ne sais où je vais,
O toi que j'eusse aimée, ô toi qui le savais!

29. *A la Recherche du temps perdu,* 1:856; 1:915-16: "Ses yeux, même fixes, donnaient l'impression de la mobilité, comme il arrive par ces jours de grand vent où l'air, quoique invisible, laisse percevoir la vitesse avec laquelle il passe sur le fond de l'azur. Un instant ses regards croisèrent les miens, comme ces ciels voyageurs de jours d'orage qui approchent d'une nuée moins rapide, la côtoient, la touchent, la dépassent. Mais ils ne se connaissent pas et s'en vont loin l'un de l'autre. Tels, nos regards furent un instant face à face, ignorant chacun ce que le continent céleste qui était devant lui contenait de promesses et de menaces pour l'avenir. Au moment seulement où son regard passa exactement sous le mien, sans ralentir sa marche, il se voila légèrement. Ainsi, par une nuit claire, la lune emportée par le vent passe sous un nuage et voile un instant son éclat, puis reparaît bien vite."

30. Ibid., 3:979-80; 3:1027-28: "Née presque sur les marches d'un trône, mariée trois fois, entretenue, longtemps et richement, par de grands banquiers, sans compter les mille fantaisies qu'elle s'était offertes, elle portait légèrement sous sa robe, mauves comme ses yeux admirables et ronds et comme sa figure fardée, les souvenirs un peu embrouillés de ce passé innombrable. Comme elle passait devant moi en se sauvant *à l'anglaise,* je la saluai. Elle me reconnut, elle me serra la main et fixa sur moi les rondes prunelles mauves de l'air qui voulait dire: 'Comme il y a longtemps que nous ne nous sommes vus! Nous parlerons de cela une autre fois.' Elle me serrait la main avec force, ne se rappelant pas au juste si en voiture, un soir qu'elle me ramenait de chez la duchesse de Guermantes, il y avait eu ou non une passade entre nous. A tout hasard elle sembla faire allusion à ce qui n'avait pas été, chose qui ne lui était pas difficile puisqu'elle prenait un air de tendresse pour une tarte aux fraises, et mettait, si elle était obligée de partir avant la fin de la musique, l'air désespéré d'un abandon qui ne serait pas définitif. Incertaine d'ailleurs sur la passade avec moi, son serrement de main furtif ne s'attarda pas et elle ne me dit pas un mot. Elle me regarda seulement comme j'ai dit, d'une façon qui signifiait 'Qu'il y a longtemps!' et où

repassaient ses maris, les hommes qui l'avaient entretenue, deux guerres, et ses yeux stellaires, semblables à une horloge astronomique taillée dans une opale, marquèrent successivement toutes ces heures solennelles du passé si lointain qu'elle retrouvait à tout moment quand elle voulait vous dire un bonjour qui était toujours une excuse."

Glossary

Cross-references within the Glossary are italicized.

Actant: a class of actors sharing certain characteristic features definable in terms of teleology. The *actor* is an individual, collective (e.g., a crowd), figurative, or nonfigurative (e.g., Fate) concrete variant of the actantial invariant. The *character* is a human or anthropomorphic individuation of the actor marked by a proper name or a thematic role (e.g., father).

Analepsis: a repetition or variant of the *prolepsis*, signaling the point in the narrative at which an event takes place that had been foreseen or foretold in the prolepsis. It is an index identifying retrospectively an implicit prolepsis.

Antanaclasis: a repetition of a word with a different meaning each time. This trope is therefore a corollary of *syllepsis*. Text production by narrative derivation from a syllepsis may be achieved by transforming the syllepsis into an antanaclasis.

Apodeictic Statement: statement expressing an absolute certainty, asserting a fact as if it were absolutely demonstrable, or alluding to that fact as if it were incontrovertible in such a way that it deprives the reader of any ground to question the statement.

Cathexis: concentration or investment of the subject's psychic energy on an object (Freud's *Besetzung*).

Character: see *Actant.*

Chronotope: a narrative unit characterized by the interrelation of space and time. I restrict such units to moments, situations, relations between characters, representations of a point in space designed to suggest a point in time or vice versa, etc. I thus remain close to Bakhtin's basic definition of the term which he was first to propose as a category (see M. M. Bakhtin, *The Dialogic Imagination,* ed. Michael Holquist [Austin: Univ. of Texas Press, 1981], 84). Bakhtin himself extends its application to include all time-space features characterizing a literary genre, making it difficult to distinguish between chronotope and genre or subgenre. The term is too felicitously precise to be so broadly generalized.

Code: a conventional system of arbitrarily chosen symbols (e.g., literary conventions). Here, the use of a *descriptive system* for the representation of an object other than the object to which that system's nuclear word refers.

Consecution: proceeding from one proposition or fact to another that follows from it. Any narrative sequence that either emphasizes consecution or makes it explicit privileges inference (reasoning from a known or assumed fact to something else that follows from it) and as a result increases predictability (e.g., representation of fate, suspense).

Deixis: the function of *indices;* the class of indices.

Derivation: narrative components, or descriptive sequences having their origin in a given or matrix. Text produced by transformation of the components of the given or matrix into larger or more complex equivalents. For a derivation to be a factor of literariness, it must be perceptible as a group of attention-catching forms, if not necessarily understood for what it is.

Descriptive System: the network of words, phrases and stereotyped sentences associated with one another in a metonymic relation to a kernel word to which they are subordinate. The relations between the system's components are regulated by the *sememe* of the nuclear word. The system serves as a model for any tropological transformation of its nucleus (e.g., a periphrasis, a metonymy of it), especially when a text is generated by *derivation* from that word. Any metonym within the system can become a metaphor for the whole. If the nucleus is used as a metaphor for another word, the system or segments of it may become a metaphoric equivalent for that word (see *code*).

Diegesis: the concrete actualization of narrative structures, namely, the verbal representation of space and time referred to in the narrative and through which it unfolds, as well as the verbal representation of events and characters (see Gérard Genette, *Figures III* [Paris: Seuil, 1972], 239, 280). In the case of verbal events, diegesis represents words uttered by characters as the narrator recounts them from his viewpoint and with the slant with which this viewpoint affects them, as opposed to words quoted verbatim. These, direct speech, are the object of the mimesis in the original sense of the term. What is shown or enacted is mimetic; what is told or reported is diegetic.

Ekphrasis: a description having a nonverbal work of art for its object (e.g., the literary depiction of a painting and also the figurative use of such a depiction).

Emblematic Names: family names (patronymics) that are also or that phonetically resemble, adjectives, common nouns, or combinations of the two. In the narrative such names serve to characterize their bearers and to program or anticipate their actions (e.g., in Dickens's *Little Dorrit*, the members of the Barnacle family are all bureaucrats and parasites of the body politic).

Given: the situational and linguistic starting point from which a narrative text is derived. The given is situational because all possible dramatic situations are variants of a finite number of invariants (themes, motifs, narrative structures). These situations allow for a limited number of endings further limited by genre-induced restrictions. They therefore regulate the development of the plot by orienting it towards a specific class of endings (*telos*). The actual denouement refers to this model either by realizing it or by departing from it. The given is linguistic inasmuch as it presupposes a system of signs with which readers are already familiar that the text reproduces and repeats or negates and cancels out to develop its own *idiolect*.

Idiolect: the distinctive grammatical features and lexical distribution of a text. A major factor of reader response is to perceive the idiolectic difference and identify it as a trait of the text's literariness, or as characteristic of an author if the corpus of that author's works exhibits traits common to all of them. In linguistics, idiolect designates those aspects of a person's speech pattern that cannot be attributed to the influence of the group or groups to which that person belongs. It is useful to distinguish idiolect from style since the former does not depend on intention nor can it be the basis of esthetic evaluation as style can. In extreme cases, an idiolect's grammar is valid only for the text in which it is observed. Most idiolects contain many features unchanged from the *sociolect*. Their own idiosyncrasies have then a literary effect as departures from these. Within the text's idiolect, the contrasting mimesis of a *character's* idiolect is a technique of portrayal. In the history of literature, convention has at times excluded such characterizations. Conversely, convention may identify them as markers of genres.

Index: a sign signifying its object solely by virtue of being connected to it (C. S. Peirce, *Collected Papers* [Cambridge: Harvard Univ. Press, 1933], 3:361). The index asserts nothing and merely points to the object it denotes (e.g., a pointing finger, a demonstrative pronoun). A full-fledged sign such as a symbol may point to the fictionality of a story irrespective of its symbolic content.

Interpretant: a sign stands for an object and creates in the mind of its interpreter an equivalent or more developed sign, the interpretant (see C. S. Peirce, *Collected Papers* [Cambridge: Harvard Univ. Press, 1933], 2:228; U. Eco, *The Role of the Reader* [Bloomington: Indiana Univ. Press, 1980], 180–99). In literature, a subtext may be a sign that stands for an intertext and its interpretant may be already actualized in yet another intertext.

Mimesis: see *Diegesis*.

Mise en Abyme: see *Subtext*.

Paradigm: a class of objects mutually substitutable in the same context. In literary theory, a class of words that can be substituted for one another in the same syntagm (e.g., synonyms, antonyms). A literary text can be generated by unfolding a paradigm of variants of its initial *given* (e.g., words or phrases that are tautologically referring to or repeating that given) along a linear sequence of successive syntagms. The paradigm then assumes the linearity that is normally a distinctive trait of syntagms (e.g., a tautological sequence).

Patronymics: see *Emblematic Names*.

Proairesis: choices faced by a character at every point in a story (Aristotle). They are defined, restricted, and even dictated by the context, the *telos*, the expectations allowed by the genre, the nature of the character, etc. An elementary and general proairesis is the choice between acting and not acting. Proairesis restricts options and is therefore a factor of narrative predictability (see Claude Bremond, *Logique du récit*, [Paris, Seuil, 1973]).

Prolepsis: any segment of a narrative that either explicitly announces a future event or is remembered when this event takes place as having foretold it or as having implicitly or figuratively anticipated it. The narrative segment that triggers this memory is the *analepsis*. An implicit or figurative prolepsis therefore has two functions: diegetic when first encountered in its own context and proleptic when reread retrospectively as an analogon of the analepsis.

Semanalysis: transformation of a unit of meaning into a larger one (usually of a word into a text) through a successive actualization of that unit's constitutive *semes* in the shape of words or phrases. Each abstract seme is concretized descriptively and narratively (from definition to description, from description to *consecution*).

Seme: a distinctive semantic feature of a *sememe* (e.g., *human* and *female* in the sememe *woman*).

Sememe: the content unit corresponding to a minimal sign or morpheme. It is a set of *semes* (e.g., the sign *bachelor*, in a narrative

excluding the academic scene or any allusion to studies corresponds to a sememe comprised of the semes *human, male, adult,
never married,* etc.). In narratology, the importance of the concept
is due to the generative powers of the seme: the sememe is an
inchoate text. Conversely, a text can be seen as an expanded
sememe (U. Eco, *The Role of the Reader* [Bloomington: Indiana
Univ. Press, 1979], 175) by virtue of the substitutability principle.
Two added features, the time dimension and *consecution,* transform such an expansion into a narrative.

Semiosis: the three-way relationship between a sign, its object, and
its *interpretant* (C. S. Peirce, *Collected Papers* [Cambridge: Harvard
Univ. Press, 1933], 5:484). It is therefore opposed to referentiality,
the assumed relationship between a sign and nonverbal objects
taken to be reality. Because the interpretant is a sign as well, it in
turn needs its own interpretant to achieve anew the three-way relationship. This process continues *ad infinitum,* thus defining unlim-
ited semiosis (see U. Eco, *A Theory of Semiotics* [Bloomington:
Indiana Univ. Press, 1976], 69, 121). This process accounts for the
self-sufficiency of a narrative *derivation* from a verbal matrix, and
also for the circularity of the semiosis when it returns to the original interpretant of a verbal sequence. It also accounts for the substitution of several signs for one, resulting in the generation of a
text equivalent to and substituted for a matrix word (see *Substitutability Principle*).

Sociolect: language both as grammar and repository of the myths,
traditions, ideological and esthetic stereotypes, commonplaces,
and themes harbored by a society, a class, or a social group. Literary texts exploit the sociolect as does any other utterance, shaping
their own original usage (*idiolect*) in conformity or in contradis-
tinction to the sociolect. Aside from syntactic structures, the sociolect contains ready-made narrative and descriptive models that
reflect a group's idea of or consensus about reality. Verisimilitude
depends on references to such models.

Substitutability Principle: the basic principle of literariness both
in *tropology* and in the generative processes that make the literary
text a unit of significance. Tropology: any trope or figure substi-

tutes an expression for another wording that it presupposes. The reader either fully reconstitutes the displaced wording or perceives the presupposition itself as an *index* of figurality. Generative process: a text can be understood as the *transformation* into larger and more complex components of a simpler initial predication that may be explicit (the *given*) or presupposed (the matrix). The text's significance is the meaning of that matrix when repeated with each successive transformation as a consistent modifier of the transformation's own discrete meanings.

Subtext: a text within a text. From the viewpoint of the text in which it appears, a subtext is a unit of significance. From the viewpoint of the readers whom it helps to perceive and decode the significance of long narratives, the subtext is a unit of reading that is a hermeneutic model (cf. 54–55, 58–59, 63–64, 99, and 110–11). It is not a subplot and must not be confused with a theme, for it has no existence outside the text in which it appears. A subtext is usually strung along the main narrative line in separate successive variants that may overlap with other subtexts. The story it tells and the objects it describes refer symbolically and metalinguistically to the novel as a whole or to some aspect of its significance. The subtext reflects the entire fiction when its structure is identical to the matrix of the novel: this is the phenomenon French theorists have called *mise en abyme* (a term of heraldry designating at the center of a coat of arms an area containing the essential bearings of the escutcheon and summarizing its symbolism) or specular texts (L. Dällenbach, *The Mirror in the Text* [Cambridge: Polity Press, 1989]).

Syllepsis: the trope that consists in using one word with two mutually incompatible meanings without repeating that word. One meaning is acceptable in the context in which the word appears; the other meaning is valid only in the intertext to which the word also belongs and which it represents at the surface of the text as the tip of the intertextual iceberg. The syllepsis is a mere phonetic shape that is filled in turn by two otherwise alien universes of representation (see 77ff.).

Telos: the limited options for and restrictive means towards the denouement of a plot allowed by the narrative given and by the genre to which the narrative belongs.

Transformation: see *Substitutability Principle.*

Tropology: literally, figurative language. More specifically, the substitution of tropes for syntactic structures (e.g., replacing a predication or organizing a sequence of phrases or sentences).

Index

Linguistic competence, 13
Literariness, xx
Lyric, 27

Marker, 7, 20, 29
Matrix, 36, 49, 55
Melville, Herman, xxi
Meredith, George, 21–28
Metalanguage, xxi, xxii, 47–48, 53, 71, 73–74, 77, 85; fictionality index, 29, 33, 46; of text, subtext as, 28
Metaphor, sustained, 45, 54, 61–63, 72
Metonymy, 5, 7, 12, 14–15, 26–28, 31, 35, 39, 41, 45, 49, 64, 67, 74
Miller, Henry, 88
Mimesis, xix, 33, 34, 37, 56, 59, 60, 80, 81, 103, 105; Aristotelian acceptation, 72–73; opposed to symbolic discourse, 82, 95; verisimilitude as specific instance of, 2, 102
Mise en abyme, 22
Mnemonic function, xxiii, 55, 63
Model, xxii, xxiii
Molière, 39
Motif, 55, 59, 88, 103

Narratology, xvii, 2, 21, 30, 31
Narrator, xviii, xxi, 41, 45, 48–49, 52, 60–61, 73, 82, 89, 91–92, 101, 105
Naturalist movement, 37

Object, 12, 56, 60; of description, 58; libidinal, 14, 20, 41, 78, 80, 86–87, 103; sign's referent, 13, 16, 26, 39, 69–70
Overdetermination, 26; role of, in verisimilitude, xxii, 7–8, 34; sub-

stitutive, 69–77; sylleptic, 70, 77–83
Oxymoron, 1, 34, 36, 42, 44, 74, 89

Paradigm, xix, 10, 43–45, 46, 98; climax of, 39–44; subtext, 110; tautological, 19–20, 27, 34, 55, 64, 85
Parody, 30, 35, 39–40, 68
Patronymics, 33–37
Peirce, Charles Sanders, 13
Periphrasis, 32, 62, 70, 77, 107; semiosis as tool of, 14, 16–19; substitution for word, 8, 12–13, 18
Performative, xix, 19, 110
Picturesque, 4, 15, 17, 95
Plautus, 38
Portrayal. *See* Character
Predication, 7, 20, 85, 87; matrix, 36–37, 74, 89; as unit of semiotic transformation, 15, 45, 102
Presupposition, xxiv, 28, 40–41, 85
Proairesis, 3–4, 32, 43, 74
Production of narrative, 20. *See* Derivation; Overdetermination
Prolepsis, 29, 63, 74
Proust, Marcel, xxiv, 8, 37–40, 49–52, 62–63, 77, 96–97, 98, 100–104, 106
Psychoanalysis, xxii–xxiii, 96, 100–103. *See* Unconscious
Pun, 34, 79

Quotation, xxi, 34, 47, 55, 100

Rabelais, François, xxi
Realism, 4, 9, 26, 58
Reference/Referent, xix, 28, 33, 47, 51, 86

Library of Congress Cataloging-in-Publication Data

Riffaterre, Michael.
Fictional truth / Michael Riffaterre.
p. cm. — (Parallax : re-visions of culture and society)
ISBN 0-8018-3933-5 (alk. paper). — ISBN 0-8018-3934-3 (pbk. : alk.
paper)
1. Fiction—History and criticism. 2. Narration
(Rhetoric) 3. Truth in literature. 4. Reality in
literature. 5. Discourse analysis, Narrative. 6. Semiotics and
literature. I. Title. II. Series: Parallax (Baltimore, Md.)
PN335.R5 1990
809.3'912—dc20   89-45491
CIP

Designed by Chris L. Hotvedt
Composed by A. W. Bennett, Inc., in Garamond Antiqua text and display
Printed by the Maple Press Company, Inc., on 55-lb. Antique Cream paper